# The American History Series

SERIES EDITORS

John Hope Franklin, *Duke University*
Abraham S. Eisenstadt, *Brooklyn College*

Donald R. Wright
STATE UNIVERSITY OF NEW YORK
COLLEGE AT CORTLAND

# African Americans in the Colonial Era

## From African Origins through the American Revolution

HARLAN DAVIDSON, INC.
WHEELING, ILLINOIS 60090-6000

**Library of Congress Cataloging-in-Publication Data**
Wright, Donald
    African Americans in the colonial era: from African origins through the American Revolution

    (The American history series)
    Includes bibliographical references.
    Includes index.
    1. Afro-Americans—History—To 1863. 2. Slavery—United States History. 3. United States—History—Colonial period, ca. 1660–1775. I. Title. II. Series: American history series (Harlan Davidson, Inc.)
    E185.W94        1990        973'.0496073—dc20            89-23633
    ISBN 0-88295-832-1

Cover illustration courtesy of the Schomburg Center for Research in Black Culture, the New York Public Library, Astor, Lenox, and Tilden Foundations.

Frontispiece reproduced from *A History of the Negro in America* by Langston Hughes and Milton Metzler, 3d. rev. ed., New York 1968; by permission from Crown Publishers, a division of Random House, Inc.

Cover design: Roger Eggers

Manufactured in the United States of America
01 00 99 98 97 6 MG

# FOREWORD

Every generation writes its own history, for the reason that it sees the past in the foreshortened perspective of its own experience. This has certainly been true of the writing of American history. The practical aim of our historiography is to offer us a more certain sense of where we are going by helping us understand the road we took in getting where we are. If the substance and nature of our historical writing is changing, it is precisely because our own generation is redefining its direction, much as the generation that preceded us redefined theirs. We are seeking a newer direction, because we are facing new problems, changing our values and premises, and shaping new institutions to meet new needs. Thus, the vitality of the present inspires the vitality of our writing about our past. Today's scholars are hard at work reconsidering every major field of our history: its politics, diplomacy, economy, society, mores, values, sexuality, and status, ethnic, and race relations. No less significantly, our scholars are using newer modes of investigation to probe the ever-expanding domain of the American past.

Our aim, in this American History Series, is to offer the reader a survey of what scholars are saying about the central themes and issues of American history. To present these themes and issues, we have invited scholars who have made notable contributions to the respective fields in which they are writing. Each volume offers the reader a sufficient factual and narrative account for perceiving the larger dimensions of its particular subject. Addressing their respective themes, our authors have undertaken, moreover, to present the conclusions derived by the principal writers on these themes. Beyond that, the authors present their own conclusions about those aspects of their respective subjects that have been matters of difference and controversy. In effect, they have written not only about where the subject stands in today's historiography but also about where they stand on their subject. Each volume closes with an extensive critical essay on the writings of the major authorities on its particular theme.

The books in this series are designed for use in both basic and advanced courses in American history. Such a series has a particular utility in times such as these, when the traditional format of our American history courses is being altered to accommodate a greater diversity of texts and reading materials. The series offers a number of distinct advantages. It extends and deepens the dimensions of course work in American history. In proceeding beyond the confines of the traditional textbook, it makes clear that the study of our past is, more than the student might otherwise infer, at once complex, sophisticated, and profound. It presents American history as a subject of continuing vitality and fresh investigation. The work of experts in their respective fields, it opens up to the student the rich findings of historical inquiry. It invites the student to join, in major fields of research, the many groups of scholars who are pondering anew the central themes and problems of our past. It challenges the student to participate actively in exploring American history and to collaborate in the creative and rigorous adventure of seeking out its wider reaches.

*John Hope Franklin*
*Abraham S. Eisenstadt*

# CONTENTS

# ACKNOWLEDGMENTS

My biggest debt is to the group of scholars, mostly historians, who, over the last two decades, produced the remarkable body of work upon which I base this study. I intended to give them individual recognition here, but the list of authors ended up resembling an abridged bibliography. So I ask the reader to examine the bibliographical essay at the end of the book, to make note of the path-breaking studies that have appeared over the last twenty years, and to know that I hold the authors of these books in high regard and offer them the gratitude of those, like me, who have followed them to a much clearer understanding of the African American past.

Several people were instrumental in bringing me to a position where I could write this book. These include my mother and father, Richard M. and Wilma S. Wright; my mentor and good friend, George E. Brooks; and Robert H. Ferrell, who cared about my writing.

Others were helpful in more specific ways. I am grateful to the editors of this series, John Hope Franklin and Abraham S. Eisenstadt, for useful suggestions—including an important one concerning broadening the original topic; to Maureen Gilgore Hewitt and Andrew J. Davidson for the right mixture of patience and encouragement, and for exceptional editorial assistance; to John C. Stockwell and Francis R. Czerwinski for helping me find time for reading and writing in a busy schedule; to Berchie S. Rafferty for leading me through the wiles of word processing; to Leonard Cohen and Eileen G. Williams for obtaining books and articles I needed; to Sidney R. Waldron for helping me gain a clearer understanding of African cultures; to C. Ashley Ellefson, Jane Landers, and Joseph C. Miller for letting me review their work before its publication (and to Landers for providing me additional information on blacks in Spanish Florida); to anonymous reviewers for detailed and careful criticism that led me to write a much better book; to my brother Dave for useful editorial suggestions on the first chapter; to Jeffrey T. Beal, Douglas A. DeRancy, Sanford J. Gutman, and Hugh Gratz for important support at different stages of my work; and to Marilou McLaughlin for reading every word, for no end of editing, and generally for making this whole project sing.

My sons, John and Ben, put up with me through the time I worked on this project. I know each missed out on something because I was writing—or suffered because I was cranky because I was not writing. I appreciate their indulgence and I will forever relish their affection.

*Donald R. Wright*

For Marilou

An advertisement of a cargo of slaves aboard the *Bance-Island*, anchored off Charleston, during a plague of smallpox.

# INTRODUCTION

For as long as professional historians have been examining America's past, the study of African Americans in slavery has been out of temporal and geographical balance. African American chattel slavery existed as a legal institution in this country for about two hundred years, roughly from the middle of the seventeenth to the middle of the nineteenth century. Most of this time—about two-thirds of it—was the colonial period of American history. From before 1650 to after 1790, American slavery occurred mainly on the plantations and smaller farms around the Chesapeake Bay in Virginia and Maryland, and throughout the coastal low country of South Carolina and Georgia. In only the last fifty years of its existence in this country did slavery move into the lands of the Deep South and undergo a switch from use predominately in tobacco or rice production to cotton. Yet the focus of the study of American slavery—and indeed of the history of all African Americans before the Civil War—has long been on the institution as it operated in the cotton South between about 1830 and 1860. The best-known books of recent years on slavery or slave society in America—Kenneth Stampp's *The Peculiar Institution: Slavery in the Antebellum South* (1956), John Blassingame's *The Slave Community: Plantation Life in the Antebellum South* (1972), Eugene Genovese's *Roll, Jordan, Roll: The*

*World The Slaves Made* (1972)—are examinations of antebellum slavery with its center in the Deep South.

That disproportionate attention from scholars has occurred largely because of the relative abundance of available historical evidence does not lessen the effect. The presentation of American slavery in high school and college textbooks and, consequently, the image of slavery that most educated Americans hold lack perspective of time and place. When considering slavery in American history, most people think of enormous plantations in Alabama or Mississippi, of persons of African descent living in quarters resembling small villages, of slaves working in gangs picking cotton, and of their efforts to escape toward the free states in the North. All of these are concepts pertinent to the Deep South in the middle of the nineteenth century. They do not reflect the lives of African Americans during the two hundred years before the rise of the Cotton Kingdom.

This study is an effort toward righting that imbalance by examining the experience of African Americans throughout the colonial era. It begins in Africa, for the African heritage has always been one of the most important factors in shaping the lives of African Americans. It examines the variety of living conditions and social relationships in Africa that formed the basis for African American culture. Then, in some detail, it addresses a topic that seldom gets attention in works of American history, the institution that brought Africans to America, the Atlantic slave trade, including particular consideration of how that trade operated on the African continent. This study then turns to the lives of African Americans in the English colonies of mainland North America, from their first arrival in 1619 to the last decade of the eighteenth century, when the infant United States was getting on its feet and black chattel slavery was further entrenched in the country's legal system. In its coverage of blacks in America through roughly one and two-thirds centuries, the study focuses on three major topics. One is the origins and development of slavery and racism in the colonies. Slavery began in different ways, at different times, in the Chesapeake Bay region, the Carolina and Georgia low country, and New England and the Middle Colonies. Some degree of racism existed before the first Africans were sold into colonial Virginia, but the fact of having African Americans and no one else in the legally defined, debased position of slavery broadened and strengthened the existing racial prejudice.

Another major topic is the beginnings and early manifestations of African American culture. The process of culture formation varied, too, according to time and place. Blacks in America first had to have extensive social contacts with other blacks—they had to exist in black communities—before they could develop group values, ways, and beliefs. Because of demographic configurations and living and working conditions, it took a long time for black communities to exist in the colonies. Once they did, the African American family became important in passing down and perpetuating manifestations of black culture.

The third major topic is the considerable changes African Americans experienced during the tumultuous quarter century of the Revolutionary era. The Revolution raised basic questions on the morality of slavery, for, after all, the Founding Fathers justified their break with England on the self-evident truth that all men are created equal. The Revolutionary era led to the ending of slavery in states north of Maryland and considerable manumission in the Upper South, while making slavery more strongly entrenched and the lives of all blacks more restricted in the states where slavery remained. The Revolutionary era also brought new strength to the racist justification for slavery and second-class citizenship for African Americans that would plague them and their descendants for more than two centuries after the Revolution had run its course.

In addition to these three major topics, three major ideas are central to this study. One is simply that a wide variety of experiences characterized the lives of blacks between the time of their existence in Africa and their living as African Americans in the United States near the end of the eighteenth century. These experiences differed considerably over time (several hundred years) and across space (within the broad expanse of western Africa itself, across the Atlantic, and within the English colonies of mainland North America). Where possible, this study emphasizes the temporal and geographical variety of these experiences.

A second idea is that blacks in western Africa through the slave trade years and blacks in America through colonial times were different sorts of people than the older racist or romantic portrayals led people to believe. Speaking generally, these Africans and African Americans were neither candidates for the objective case, always being done unto and never doing, nor wily calculators, always thinking of ways to dupe their masters. They were normal human beings with complex characters who made rational decisions under varied and difficult circumstances. We are fortunate to be at a stage in the continually evolving study of African American history when we can step away from stereotypes and exaggerations and emphasize the humanity of blacks.

A third idea is that through the long period of evolution of slavery and black society in the colonial period, much of the course for the subsequent history of African Americans was set. By 1790 the basic American institutions and attitudes concerning slavery and racism were established, and by that same time the forces were in motion that would lead to the expansion of slavery, the struggle that would fuel sectionalism and help bring on the Civil War, and the rapid move toward second-class citizenship for African Americans following the legal demise of slavery in 1865. Also, by 1790 the most important elements of African American culture—family, religion, a spirit of resistance, and a host of truly African American ways of living—were set firmly in a stable black community. From this base, the African American community and culture would evolve through the next two centuries, over which time they would provide African Americans an identity and help them cope with a hostile world. Thus, in the broadest sense, the colonial era encompassed the truly formative years of the African American experience.

# CHAPTER ONE

# Atlantic Origins

In the spring of 1727 an English barque, the *John and Betty*, sailed up Chesapeake Bay and into the mouth of the Rappahannock River with 140 African slaves on board. The ship's master, William Denton, brought the vessel to anchor off the main wharf of Robert "King" Carter's enormous plantation. Denton called on Carter and got the planter to manage the sale of the slaves.

For three weeks Carter rowed daily to the barque, where he held forth with fellow planters, dealing for the slaves. The cargo was smaller than many straight from Guinea, so it was not of extraordinary value. Still, it was early in tobacco-growing season and demand was high. Also, a number of the Africans were from Senegambia and the Gold Coast, the areas Virginia planters favored most. So on typical days Carter sold half a dozen slaves, often in pairs, at from £12 to £20 each. When he finished he was wealthier from his percentage of each transaction, and he was convinced he had performed a service for the plantation economy of tidewater Virginia.

Less noticeable than all the Carters in the historical record, the 140 Africans, who were scattered about the area, proceeded to learn their work. They were part of the labor force of the eighteenth-century British colonies on the North American mainland. If they survived long under the difficult conditions of their new environment, they would begin the lengthy process of acculturation that would make them and their descendants African Americans.

What occurred on the Rappahannock in 1727 took place in varied fashion over several centuries along the Atlantic side of the New World, from the British colonies in the north to Brazil in the south. The colonies were part of an enormous economic system that linked the continents bordering the Atlantic Ocean. The system relied on European management, capital, and shipping, and it involved New World production of goods for European consumption. By the seventeenth century those in control of the system preferred African slaves for the colonial labor force.

The idea of importing labor from some distance for intensive work on export crops was an old one. From the thirteenth century a plantation system had existed in the eastern Mediterranean, geared to provide a European market with sugar. Like the Atlantic plantations of half a millennium later, capital and management came from Europe and labor to grow the cane was human property. Mediterranean shippers brought in workers from southern Russia (thus the word *slave*, from Slav), the eastern Mediterranean, and North Africa. For over two centuries the plantations made profits and the institution spread. By 1450, on the eve of European expansion into the south Atlantic, sugar plantations existed in the western Mediterranean and even on nearby Atlantic islands.

The Europeans who ventured away from their homelands after the middle of the fifteenth century and established outposts or acquired vast lands on both sides of the Atlantic had less selfless motives than spreading Christianity or increasing geographical knowledge. Many wanted to become wealthy. This was not difficult in the lands that held gold and silver, but most of the lands bordering the Atlantic did not. So the new occupants turned to export production, with sugar as the focus. A model for doing so already existed. Thus developed an Atlantic agricultural economy, first on some African islands and then, by the end of the sixteenth century, on land in north-eastern Brazil. By 1640 a staple-export economy had spread to the Lesser Antilles in the Caribbean and, on a smaller scale, to English tobacco-growing colonies on the North American mainland. As the Atlantic economy expanded, the plantation model, on a larger scale than ever before, became the accepted way of making profits from the expanse of land.

Establishing plantations was not easy. Sugar remained in great demand, the land would produce, the technology existed, but finding workers for the labor-intensive crop became a problem. Those native to America, the so-called Indians, never worked out as the landowners had hoped. Native Americans died too rapidly in captivity from the Old World diseases of smallpox, mumps, and measles that Europeans brought to the Americas. Also, Indians ran away with ease, for their homes were usually close by. Bonded Europeans, usually criminals sentenced to labor or men under indentures to gain passage and opportunity, were not a great deal better. White laborers fell victim to diseases too, mostly to tropical malaria and yellow fever, and they could run away and pass as members of the ruling society.

But Africans were different in important ways, and European planters soon recognized the differences, even if they did not understand why they existed. The African homelands of black slaves were places where Old World diseases and tropical diseases were endemic. Africans who survived into adolescence acquired some immunity to smallpox, mumps, and measles *and* to malaria and yellow fever. So in the fresh mix of diseases of the New World plantation environment, Africans lived longer—three to five times longer than their white counterparts. They were thus able to produce more. Also, when Africans ran away they could neither run home nor be mistaken for a member of the society of planters. And through most of the years of the Atlantic trade, prices for Africans remained favorable in relation to the price of the crops they produced. (For example, an English planter on the Caribbean island of Jamaica in 1690 had to pay £20 for a "prime" male African, direct from Guinea. That laborer could produce about five hundred pounds of sugar in a year. The planter could sell the five hundred pounds of sugar for £20, and thus in a year recover the original cost of the slave.) In short, African laborers turned out to be the best deal in economic terms, which were the only terms of real interest to the landowners, shippers, financiers, and merchants involved in the plantation system.

## The African Background

Slaves came to the British mainland colonies over one of two general routes. One was from the West Indies and normally involved shippers of general merchandise, who topped off their cargos with slaves as opportunities offered. Many ships came to the colonies so laden, but they brought relatively few slaves—about 15 percent of the total. The overwhelming number of slave imports, roughly four of every five, arrived directly from Africa. These newcomers were unacculturated, raw, frightened—sometimes called "outlandish"—persons not long away from their African homes.

Nearly all slaves brought to English North America came from the coast and interior of western and west-central Africa. A few came from the Mozambique coast or Madagascar, around the Cape of Good Hope. English traders brought 85 percent of all slaves arriving in the mainland colonies, and the English, never developing close, long-standing links with specific African regions for their slaves, purchased captives all along about thirty-five hundred miles of African coastline from Senegal in the north to Angola in the south. Yet some African markets were especially important as sources for English slaves through the years of the heaviest importing into North America. About a quarter of slave imports to the colonies came from the hinterland of the coastal region normally designated

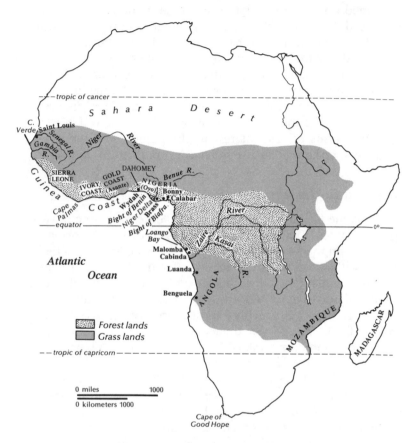

Africa in the Era of the Atlantic Trade,
Seventeenth and Eighteenth Centuries

"Congo-Angola," the portion within five hundred miles north or south of the Zaire (formerly the Congo) River. Portuguese merchants dominated the southern portion of this trade and carried most of their slaves to Brazil, but English and Dutch slavers frequented the ports north of the Zaire and brought many Kongo, Tio, and Matamba slaves to North America. Later in the eighteenth century more slaves came to English colonies from the Portuguese ports of Luanda and Benguela and thus were from such groups as the Ovimbundu and Kwanza. Another quarter came from the coast of southeastern Nigeria, primarily the lands of the Ibo and Ibibio. About 15 percent each came from Senegambia, the land between and around the Senegal and Gambia rivers (Mandinka, Fulbe, Serer, Wolof, Bambara, and Jola); the Gold Coast (Ashanti, Fanti); and the coast between and including Sierra Leone and Ivory Coast (Vai, Mende, Kpelle, Kru).

The lands of western Africa's Atlantic zone are among the continent's most livable. The population of these lands diminished or grew with droughts and famines or periods of abundance, but it seems generally to have been substantial back through the centuries. At the heart of the region are the rain forests of the Guinea Coast and Zaire River basin. Here proximity to the equator keeps the region under the influence of tropical convergence zones that generate regular and often bountiful rainfall. Vegetation is lush in spite of the compact soils. Palms and hardwoods abound, overshadowing smaller growth that competes for sunlight filtering through the trees. As one moves away from the equator, rainfall diminishes and so does plant life. North of the Guinea Coast, forests give way gradually to wooded savanna, and the farther north one travels the less dense is the ground cover. Across the central belt of West Africa stretches the enormous sky and seemingly endless horizons that make up the broad reaches of the Western Sudan. This is the land that inspired British colonials to write home about "miles and miles of bloody Africa." The population sustains itself with a combination of agriculture and pastoralism—farming and herding. Farther north still, rolling grasslands peppered with trees become drier until vegetation grows sparse. North African Arabs called this dry zone the *Sahel*, the southern "shore" of the Sahara Desert. It sustains a small population of pastoralists who move their herds with the rainfall.

Similarly, to the south the Congo forests blend gradually into the southern savannas, and even into desert below Angola. Rains come to both savanna areas seasonally, through their respective summer months, when vegetation takes on new life and crops thrive. Human life is not so healthy during the rains, however, for disease-spreading mosquitos come out in profusion, with standing ponds and puddles for breeding grounds. Back through time it was in the dry season, when crops were in and lands dried out, that the savannas saw more travel, long-distance trade, and, no doubt, warfare.

Any broad discussion of the lives of Africans prior to their enslavement and shipment to America has to misrepresent the way things were. African societies differed greatly to begin with, and they changed over time. The peoples of western and west-central Africa spoke several hundred mutually unintelligible languages (or dialects thereof) and practiced social customs that, in some extremes, were as different from one another as they were from those of Europeans. Furthermore, the English colonies of North America imported Africans for over 150 years, and African societies changed as much over this time as did the American society the slaves entered. Life in, say, Angola in 1650 was different in many ways from life in Senegal at the same time, just as it was different from life in Angola in 1800. So the task of describing the "African background" of African Americans seems even more difficult than describing "life in America" from 1607 to 1787.

Still, in a broad sense, black Africans from the slave-trading area exhibited some elements of cultural homogeneity through the seventeenth and eighteenth centuries, much as they did before and after. Most identified primarily with family and descent groups. An extended family occupying a section of a village was the group that lived and worked together. West Africans tended to trace descent through the male side of the family while west-central and central Africans followed matri-lineal descent. Most practiced polygyny, with wealthier men having more wives and larger families. Security was in num-bers of kinsmen and in stores of food or animals on the hoof. Although large centers for trade existed, particularly in some of the interior river towns and some ports on the Atlantic coast, small villages were common throughout the whole region. Vil-lagers worked out a sense of community and cooperation that enabled them to gain the most security and pleasure from their varied situations.

The vast majority of these black Africans also relied on one of the basic modes of subsistence: pastoralism or agricul-ture. Herdsmen kept cattle, sheep, or goats on the northern and southern extremes of the Atlantic's slave-gathering area, where rainfall was not sufficient for growing crops. Farmers of the savannas north or south of the equatorial forests grew dry rice, millet, or maize—the latter brought by the Portuguese from the New World by 1600. Those of the more heavily wooded areas nearer the equator grew yams and manioc or harvested bananas, plantains, or palm products. Some of these distinctions are not so important when one considers that Sen-egalese millet farmers, Nigerian yam farmers, and Angolan maize farmers used similar methods of cultivation, mostly variations of slash-and-burn, or that herders of the savannas often lived in close, symbiotic relationships with grain farmers, exchanging products from their animals (including dung for fuel and fertilizer) for foodstuffs for themselves and their herds and flocks.

Yet in many places local identity, local customs, and lan-guage differences tempered a broad sense of unity. Modern maps that show large language families spanning great stretches of the savannas and forests fail to give a complete picture of black Africa's linguistic diversity. Many of the lan-guages were spoken only by small groups, and some of the most widely spoken languages were divided into a number of dialects that far fewer people spoke and understood. There was even greater political difference, a fact that the large conquest states or "empires" of earlier or later times often mask. In no sense of the word did black Africans identify themselves as members of a "tribe" and thus take their places in a large socio-political realm of "tribal Africa." Colonial officials, early anthropologists, museum curators, and other makers of "tribal" maps have created that false sense, and it is one that dies hard. Individual allegiances were normally to the extended family and the village. Sometimes the allegiances carried more broadly, and nebulously, to a descent group or clan; sometimes they spread even beyond, especially when forced, to a larger political unit—a state or an empire. Certainly relations existed among and across political and language boundaries. Long-distance traders moved across political boundaries, religions and secret societies spread and provided a commonality in larger areas, and historical events united groups of Africans. But most frequently blacks from western and west-central Africa had a restricted definition of their own group. General outlooks were local. "We" included the people of the lineage, the village, the small political unit. "They" included everyone else.

Among many of the pastoral and agrarian societies of western and west-central Africa, slavery had long been an established social and economic institution. Although practice of slavery varied considerably among African societies, and through time, there is no doubt of its importance. In some regions of west Africa in the nineteenth century, slaves made up three-quarters of the population. It was different from the chattel slavery of the Western world, however. Almost everywhere it existed slavery was tied to kinship systems. African societies typically relied on a form of labor organization called the "domestic mode of production." A person's household was the work unit. Households got wealthier by producing more; they produced more by bringing more workers to the task of production; and they got more workers by increasing the size of the household. This they could do over time through marriage and procreation, but they could accomplish it more rapidly by adding dependents to the family by other means. Such dependency could take several forms. Slavery was one. The addition of slaves to a household increased its power and prestige as well as its ability to produce. Slaves did the same variety of tasks as other family members, though sometimes they specialized in a single craft, such as cloth weaving. There were typical divisions of labor along lines of gender and age. Over several generations, and increasingly with marriage and childbirth, slaves could become recognized members of the household. The difference was that slaves and their descendants were always outsiders. Thus their economic, political, or social exploitation by the insiders, the original family members, was possible. Although slaves' fortunes often rose with the position of the family upon which they depended, they never entirely lost their personal status as "other than kin."

One could find slaves, too, serving in offices of state. This was especially true in those parts of western Africa under Muslim influence. Muslims believed prisoners of war were property, and African societies that relied on Muslim institutions and advisors adopted this position. Thus, governments could use captives as they saw fit—the more acculturated, who saw the state's best interests as their own, as soldiers or administrators; the less acculturated as domestic servants or workers in such varied forms of state production as gold mining or large-scale farming.

As in most places where slavery existed, African societies obtained slaves by more or less violent means. Warfare—including raids, banditry, and kidnapping—was the most common method. Even wars not fought to gain slaves often had that effect, for prisoners of war were usually enslaved and sold or put to work to help defray the costs of the wars. If ransom was impossible, there were other considerations. Young boys could train as future soldiers; girls and women could become concubines; slaves of either sex could be given as gifts to religious persons or shrines. But generally captives were not especially valuable near their place of capture. They were close to home and likely to escape. Wise captors moved prisoners rapidly and sold them away quickly if there were no pressing needs for their labor. Even if the need for labor was strong, it was often better to sell off local captives and buy slaves from some distance away. For these reasons African armies often had a following of merchants eager to buy prisoners at low prices and then march them off to distant markets where their value would be greater.

Less violent methods of enslaving involved condemnation through judicial or religious proceedings for civil crimes or supposed religious wrongdoing. As Atlantic slaving in western Africa grew heavy, slavery probably became a more common punishment for an increasing number of offenses to society. And, finally, there is even some evidence of individuals voluntarily enslaving themselves, almost always because they could not feed or otherwise take care of themselves or their families. In the worst of times, they chose dependence over starvation.

African societies that regularly acquired slaves were also accustomed to trading them. In fact, export of slaves from black Africa had roots far deeper than the earliest individuals exported via the Atlantic. Various groups across western Africa sold slaves into the trade that led to and across the Sahara to North Africa. The trans-Sahara slave trade out of black Africa lasted longer than the Atlantic trade, from before A.D. 700 to near the beginning of the twentieth century. Over this time it was the means of exporting between eight and ten million slaves. Central Africans sold captives eastward toward the Indian Ocean for about the same length of time. All this is part of what historians now recognize as the Black Diaspora—the movement of peoples from their sub-Saharan African homes to permanent locations in lands covering half the world.

So the onset of the Atlantic trade did not signal something altogether new for western black Africans. When European demand appeared along the Atlantic coast, Africans had social and economic institutions in place to provide slaves in exchange for commodities they preferred. Little was different about trading slaves coastward instead of inland—just the shippers and their destination. However, what proved to be most novel about the Atlantic trade was its scale. No other exporting of slaves, at any time or place before or since, came close to the massive, involuntary movement of people out of western and west-central black Africa to the New World over the four centuries following 1450.

## The Atlantic Trade

The enterprise that brought African slaves to the New World, and after 1619 to the areas of the North American mainland under English control, was what most people now call the Atlantic slave trade. It was an undertaking of massive proportions in terms of duration, area, and numbers of people involved. It began shortly after 1450, with the export of African slaves to continental Europe and sugar plantations on the Atlantic islands, and lasted until after the middle of the nineteenth century. Over the course of four centuries it caused the greatest intercontinental migration in world history to that time, and it affected people and the history of their offspring on all lands bordering the Atlantic.

For many years, historians' estimates of the numbers of Africans transported across the Atlantic as part of the slave trade varied widely. Some thought in terms of a total of 20 million or more; others considered the figure to be barely a quarter of that. Most agreed it was hard to determine. Records were sparse, in several languages, and difficult to come by. But in 1969 Philip D. Curtin, a historian who had used many of the existing shipping records of the Atlantic trade, produced a monumental work, *The Atlantic Slave Trade: A Census*, which attempted to estimate the volume of the trade over time. Although Curtin's estimates generated a debate that is not yet completely resolved, many now agree on some approximate numbers that are but a slight upward revision of Curtin's original figures. In rough terms, over 11.5 million people were exported from the Atlantic coast of black Africa and nearly 10 million of these people arrived in the New World. Annual averages of Africans brought to the New World grew from about 2,000, in the late 1500s, to a peak of 80,000 in 1780. No enterprise of such proportion could have existed through casual contact or chance capture. The Atlantic slave trade was carefully planned big business.

Study of the Atlantic slave trade sometimes involves more numbers and percentages than one might wish to consider, but the numbers and percentages have their role. They are particularly important for putting parts of the trade in temporal and spatial perspective. Only a small portion of the trade brought captives to the English North American mainland. Of all the Africans who crossed the Atlantic as part of the slave trade, less than 5 percent of the total (fewer than entered the island of Cuba) came to the mainland colonies. However, because the heaviest trade to the mainland lasted only from about 1680 to 1808, that trade accounted for some 7 percent of the volume crossing the ocean through those years, and it was a much greater portion, about one-fifth, of the English slave trade at the time. In fact, through several decades after 1740 the British mainland colonies ran a close second to Jamaica as Britain's leading slave market. Thus, in spite of the relative insignificance of the total numbers, during the heaviest years of trading in the eighteenth century the mainland colonies were important markets for British slavers.

From 1650 to after 1800, demand for slaves varied at ports all along America's Atlantic seaboard, from Salem in the Massachusetts Bay colony down through Savannah in Georgia and beyond. In some years such ports as Philadelphia or New York might have imported Africans in the several hundreds. However, three zones along the Atlantic coast served as the colonies' major markets for slaves. They differed in demand and, hence, volume of imports as years passed. The earliest big market was the Chesapeake Bay that touched the coasts of Virginia and Maryland. Slaves began entering there by the shipload after 1680 and the numbers swelled into the thousands in certain years after 1720. South Carolina did not begin importing persons directly from Africa in any number until after 1700, but once it did it grew quickly to become the colonies' largest importer—at that time and eventually for all time. By the 1730s South Carolina was importing, on average, over two thousand slaves each year. The third market of significance, coastal Georgia, was a late one. Demand for workers appeared there after 1755, when planters opened new lands and wanted slave labor. But Georgia relied strictly on the reexport trade from the West Indies for its slaves until 1766, when the first vessel arrived in Savannah from the African coast. Thereafter direct and much larger shipments became the norm.

A Dutch ship brought the first Africans to the English North American mainland in 1619.* Jamestown tobacco planter John Rolfe, who recorded sundry events in the settlement, noted casually that, "About the last of August came in a dutch man of warre that sold us twenty Negars." Dutch merchants continued to play the biggest role in the relatively meager mainland slave trade through 1650. Thereafter English owned and operated vessels took over and carried the lion's share of slaves to British North America. London and Bristol were important English ports participating in the trade, but Liverpool surpassed them both as the eighteenth century ran its course. Also entering into the trafficking of slaves after the middle of the seventeenth century were colonial merchants. Beginning with New Englanders but growing to include entrepreneurs from New York, Philadelphia, and Baltimore, American shippers increased their share of English slaving to a high of perhaps one-third through the quarter century before the American Revolution. Rhode Island became the colony fitting out the largest number of vessels. Through the fifteen years prior to the American Revolution, 271 vessels cleared Rhode Island ports for the African trade, bringing to the Americas over thirty-two thousand persons.

---

* This was not the first time persons of African descent set foot on land that would become the United States. Spanish conquistadores brought African slaves with them as they sought their fortunes, and Africans served as soldiers and scouts for Spanish military operations. One African, the celebrated Estevanico, survived Panfilo de Narvaéz's 1528 expedition in Florida and then joined an eight-year trek across the continent to Mexico City.

For the first seventy-five years of the colonies' existence, slaves imported into English North America were mostly "seasoned." These men and women came from one of the islands in the Caribbean, principally Barbados or Jamaica, where they had made it through the difficult adjustment to a new disease environment and had learned enough English and enough of what their situations required of them to get by. Importation of Caribbean slaves was not so much the result of the preference of the mainland planters for seasoned workers as it was a function of the mainland market that was not yet strong enough to draw vessels with larger numbers of captives directly from Africa. But buyers in Virginia, Maryland, and South Carolina eventually recognized the tendency of island planters to unload "refuse Negroes" and "rogues" on the mainland. They also realized that slaves straight from the continent were cheaper and, because they were unacculturated, less likely to band together with other blacks and rebel. Thus, over the half century from 1680 to 1730, the source of mainland slaves changed. By 1720 the balance between "outlandish" Africans and "seasoned" West Indian imports was about equal. After 1720, four of every five slaves imported into Virginia, Maryland, the Carolinas, and Georgia arrived on a ship directly across the ocean from Africa.*

---

* The English and Spanish colonies were not the only places on the North American mainland where European colonials brought Africans and kept slaves. The French *Compagnie des Indies* imported 500 Africans into Louisiana in the summer of 1719; Africans then were instrumental in building levees and ditches to make New Orleans habitable; and through the 1720s black slaves helped create an industry of naval stores near the Gulf of Mexico and performed agricultural labor along the Mississippi to as far north as Natchez. After 1731 the French government took over the lower Mississippi, with its 1,700 European settlers and 3,600 African slaves. Dependence on African labor would grow in Louisiana through the rest of the eighteenth century. A unique set of demographic and economic conditions would eventually bring about the rise of a sizable free black population and a regular militia of African American troops. But, as Daniel H. Usner, Jr. writes in "From African Captivity to American Slavery: The Introduction of Black Laborers to Colonial Louisiana," *Louisiana History* (1979), "the overwhelming scarcity of black laborers in Louisiana created a pattern of race relations largely resembling slavery in other North American colonies."

Of course, the magnitude of the whole Atlantic trade, or even that of the trade to British North America, makes it impossible to describe the way it operated in simple generalities. Trading differed considerably along the African and American coasts. Operations were different a few hundred miles apart. Ease of procuring captives or methods of doing so could change from one year to the next, let alone over periods of half a century or more, and various African and American ports matured as slave markets at different times. Yet, through the centuries and across the boundaries of cultural areas, certain broad modes of operation seem to have persisted from shortly after the opening of the trade through the eighteenth century.

Trading slaves into the Atlantic world was always part of a larger body of exchange. Slaves were but one export commodity among a variety of trade goods. For the first two centuries of Atlantic commerce until after 1650, Europeans exported a combination of other items in greater amounts (by value), including especially gold, than slaves. Around 1700, slaves became the principal African export into the Atlantic colonies and remained so until after 1850.

From the beginning, Europeans realized they were not seeking slaves from a vast, undeveloped wilderness where savages spent their days in idleness and their nights in levity. That white traders believed such misinformation is a notion that came about long after the fact—during the persistent wave of pseudoscientific racism of the late nineteenth century. The western coast of Africa was the outward edge of a commercial network of considerable size and scope that had been in existence since the middle ages of African history. Long-distance trading was an occupational specialty that western and west-central Africans held in high regard. The Atlantic hinterland of black Africa contained a grid of trade routes dotted with regular commercial settlements. These formed a network that permitted traders to travel widely among communities where they could employ local associates as their aids and agents. For hundreds of years before the coastwise trade in slaves, itinerant merchants had funneled gold, kola nuts, and slaves to the "port" cities of the Sahel for transport across the Sahara. In return they had carried goods from North Africa, including salt, metalware and glassware, figs and dates, back from the southern edge of the desert to locales across the western savannas and into the coastal forests. Central Africans had traded copper, hides, and ivory toward the coast for palm cloth, palm oil, and salt. Once demand for slaves and other products—some of which, such as foodstuffs, were ancillary to the slave trade—became evident along the coastal periphery of the commercial network, it did not take long for the traders to extend operations to the European outposts at the mouths of rivers and on Atlantic beaches and islands. Thus, fairly rapidly, a commercial system was in place to supply products Europeans wanted and to distribute goods Africans desired in exchange.

Great temporal and regional variance characterized African products in European demand. At different times Europeans sought gold, gum, hides, ivory, and beeswax from Senegambia; gold and peppers from Sierra Leone; gold from the Gold Coast; palm products from the Niger Delta; copper, ivory, and dyewoods from the Zaire basin. Throughout the length of the coast Europeans obtained African products, kola nuts or palm cloth, for instance, to exchange elsewhere on the continent for other locally produced commodities. But all along the thirty-five hundred-mile coastline slaves were in fairly constant and growing demand after 1650. In some areas, Angola for example, slaves were almost always the principal item the Europeans wanted.

Africans were no less careful in designating the products they wanted in exchange. Meeting their varied and changing demands was a necessity for the ship captain who wanted good prices for slaves. The ships that sailed down the Guinea Coast thus had to serve as floating hardware and drygoods stores with spirits in the cellar. Africans in many locales wanted metals and metalware. They also had considerable demand for varieties of cloth, beads and semiprecious stones, and brandy or rum. Most African societies could manufacture these items, but they could not always do it so well or so inexpensively as their European counterparts. Horses for cavalry use (which, because of sleeping sickness, bred with difficulty in areas infested with the tsetse fly), cutlery, and firearms were also in greater or lesser demand, depending on local supplies and, in some areas, regional hostilities.

Whether exporting or importing, it was the mesh of the organized commercial networks that made the magnitude of the exchange possible. It is obvious that without European shipping and a considerable demand for labor on the plantations of the New World the Atlantic slave trade could not have taken place. It is less obvious, mostly because of insufficient knowledge of Africa and its history, that without the existing commercial operations in the hinterland of Africa's Atlantic coast and without sufficient African demand for European products, the supply of slaves could never have reached the massive proportions that it did.

The first Europeans to sail down the northwest coast of Africa were the Portuguese. They were the vanguard of what would be a long line of Europeans who wedded a capitalist economic system (with special desire to invest in long-distance trade) to advanced maritime technology, and they dominated foreign trade with black Africa for the first two centuries of European contact. After a few episodes in the 1440s of capturing residents of the coasts of Morocco and Mauritania by surprise and sending them back to Lisbon, Portuguese seamen and merchants came to realize what should have been obvious from the beginning: that Africans were not going to wait passively until the next vessel full of marauders arrived to fall upon their dwindling numbers; that Africans were not different from others in their interest in and willingness to exchange human beings for products they needed or wanted; and that Atlantic sailors could, therefore, more easily and safely acquire slaves by trade than by capture. It would eventually be apparent to most European traders that some African groups were powerful and would not allow European raiding on land in their vicinities, and it would be clear that Europeans could not live long enough in the tropical environment, generally speaking, to be able to maintain an effective raiding force over the long term. However, these issues did not bear on the initial decision to acquire slaves through exchange of goods. So within a few decades of Portuguese contact with black Africa, a broad pattern of European-African trade came into being that, with minor changes, would be the standard way of trading for slaves from north of the Senegal River to south of Angola until the very last years of the Atlantic trade.

With rare exceptions, the Europeans stopped at or stayed close to the waterside, leaving to the Africans the conduct of their own political and military affairs. The Europeans had little choice. Africans were insistent on maintaining their position as middlemen in the trade to the interior. Any white person who marched inland or went far upriver usually paid dearly for that temerity. But Europeans had their hands full just manning their coastal outposts and bulking stations because of the overwhelming loss of life in these places to disease. Death rates varied, but before the use of quinine (after 1850) European mortality rates in tropical Africa ranged from 250 to 750 per thousand per year. In some locales over certain years it was worse.

European governments sought initially to conduct slaving through the granting of monopolies to private, joint-stock companies. In the ideal, a single company would carry out its nation's African trade. These companies would use their inordinately large profits from the monopoly to offset the cost of maintaining fortified outposts on the coast. England, for example, attempted two such ventures, first with the Company of Royal Adventurers for nine years after 1663, and then with the better known and somewhat more successful Royal African Company from 1672 through the end of the century. But by the onset of the eighteenth century it was clear that the monopolies could not hold their own. There were too many "interlopers" trading with anyone out of gunshot of the company forts, and there were too many planters across the Atlantic wanting to pay bottom prices for workers, regardless of seller. Exclusive trade for any nation's carriers was doomed. After 1700, independent shippers carried the bulk of the trade, and the competition grew fierce with the rising demand for slaves in the New World.

The end of monopolies did not mean the end of European outposts or "factories" on western Africa's small islands, riverbanks, or ocean beaches. It was still profitable for a European nation to have places along the coast where slaves were "bulked," awaiting purchase and shipment to the New World. Slaving vessels could appear; purchase slaves on hand; obtain food, water, and firewood; and be off within a short time for American markets. Paying a hefty markup for the services was often good business. Waiting to load slaves not yet arrived from the interior or coasting along from market to market in search of a cargo was profitless dead time for the slavers— while crew and captives still had to be fed. Furthermore, time spent on the coast meant time spent in the tropical disease environment where crew and human cargo were most likely to sicken and die. In an extreme situation in the mid-eighteenth century, a ship slaving in Loango Bay north of the Zaire River needed nine months in port to acquire 348 slaves. By the time the vessel was ready to sail for the Americas, 83 of the Africans on board had died.

From Saint Louis, at the mouth of the Senegal River, to Benguela on the Angola Coast, whether under English, French, Dutch, Danish, or Portuguese flags, the outposts were similar in operation if not in form. They might be large, walled castles like the English operation at Cape Coast on the Gold Coast; they might be smaller stone forts like James Fort on a little island in the Gambia River; or they might be thatched-roof dwellings along a high-surfed Guinea beach. Most were fortified to protect against attacks from pirates and national enemies by sea. Inside the fort were living quarters for a garrison, a warehouse for trade goods, and a store for food. Inside or outside, depending on the security of the location, was a place to keep slaves until they could be loaded aboard a vessel.

Residents of the forts had to pay Africans for occupancy of their territory and were dependent on the local people for food and water. Once the outposts were established and manned, African merchants from the near and more distant interior brought slaves and other commodities for exchange. Sometimes, in Congo-Angola, caravans left for the interior from a particular outpost specifically to return with slaves. Under ideal circumstances the outpost could acquire the slaves and products of an entire caravan for goods on hand, then could hold the captives and other trade goods until a ship arrived to take on a cargo.

Around the European outposts, up and down some of the major rivers of Africa's Atlantic coast, developed small but important commercial communities that took part in the dealings. Philip D. Curtin in *Cross-Cultural Trade in World History* (1984) calls attention to such hybrid communities that have always tended to grow up around the "nodes" of contact in "trade diasporas." When the Atlantic trade came into being these communities formed around European establishments. Their commercial influence usually spread up rivers as far as fair-sized vessels could navigate, along Atlantic beaches, and to smaller outposts of their own short distances away from the major points of cross-cultural contact. In these communities were groups of people, sometimes whole families and sometimes larger groups that included aids of chiefs and rulers, who served as intermediaries, cultural and commercial brokers, between European shippers and African sellers. A number of these intermediaries were the offspring of more or less formal unions between European men (who normally came to the coast, had a child or children, and died or returned to Europe) and African women. With attachment to each cultural milieu, these Afro-Europeans were in some places the key links in the chain of production, transportation, and acquisition of slaves on the coast.

Not all slavers chose to sail to the government-subsidized or company-affiliated outposts, where the most thoroughly integrated commercial communities existed. Some sailed to reputed slaving locations along the coast and carried on much less formal dealings on board their ships. The appearance of a vessel anchored off the coast might bring one or several traders out in longboats to talk with captains about slaving prospects or to deal for slaves on hand. These traders were often Europeans, renegades of a kind who had struck out on their own to make a profit in the thriving commerce, and occasionally Africans with the same intentions. Most were Afro-Europeans though. Some of these traders were dirt poor, barely scratching out an existence, without capital, trade goods, or credit worthy of note. Others, some of the mulattos in particular, had been in the business for several generations and were the masters or mistresses of organized "trading houses" who had connections (often through marriage) with important African political and commercial leaders, had their own store of goods and foodstuffs, advanced credit to Africans and other Afro-European traders, and bulked slaves in expectation of the arrival of vessels willing to pay good prices.

Along the coast of Sierra Leone in the middle of the eighteenth century, one could encounter traders at both extremes of prosperity. Near the Sherbro region was Irishman Nicholas Owen, who ventured to Africa to recover his family's lost fortune. Of his operation, Owen admitted

... if any of the blacks comes I buy their commodities at as cheap a rate as I can, which enables me to trade aboard the ships once or twice a month, which just keeps me from sinking in the principle stock.

But from Owen's location a slaver did not have to sail far to encounter the mulatto Henry Tucker, a man who had travelled in Europe and who lived "in the English manner." Tucker had six wives and many children who participated in his operations. He even maintained his own fields with slave labor to grow provisions for slave ships. Owen describes his wealthy competitor:

His strength consists of his own slaves and their children, who have built a town about him and serve as his *gremetos* [aids in commercial dealings] upon all occasions. This man bears the character of a fair trader among the Europeans, but to the contrary among the blacks. His riches set him above the kings and his numerous people above being surprised by war; almost all the blacks owe him money, which brings a dread of being stopt upon that account, so that he is esteemed and feared by all who have the misfortune to be in his power.

Meshing with the European system in the vicinity of the outposts and ports was an African economic network of equal complexity. Throughout the hinterland of Africa's Atlantic coast there developed, over time, slave-gathering, delivery, and marketing systems that were organized, systematic, efficient, and competitive. These systems were integrated with the movement of other goods to the coast and with the dispersal of European wares brought in exchange. If no two systems were alike, they fell within general patterns of operation according to region and time of trade.

Across the western savannas, from Senegambia to Lake Chad and as far south as the central Gold Coast, slave caravans were under the control of specialized Muslim African merchants. These politically neutral "international" traders, themselves slave owners and users, relied on ethnic relations, personal connections, and a broad sense of occupational solidarity throughout the dispersed commercial communities of the trading network to ease the movement of caravans and to get the most from their trade. When Englishman Richard Jobson was trading some distance up the Gambia River in 1620, he dealt with an African trader who appealed to Jobson's feeling for fellow merchants. "In our time of trading together," Jobson writes,

if it were his owne goods he bartered for, he would tell us, this is for my self, and you must deale better with me, than either with the Kings of the Country or any others, because I am as you are, a Julietto, which signifies a Merchant, that goes from place to place, neither do I, as the Kings of our Country do which is to eate, and drinke, and lye still at home among their women, but I seeke abroad as you doe.

Caravans of a thousand persons and scores of pack animals trekked across hundreds of miles of west Africa's savannas. The caravan leader was responsible for the arrangements—credit especially, but also food, protection, and local trading. Agents in towns along the way lent assistance. Such aid was vital to the success of a large caravan where problems of provisioning were like those of a small army and where local officials charged variable tariffs and tolls. When known agents were not available, caravan leaders relied on West Africa's centuries-old, institutional custom of hospitality and reciprocity, the "landlord-stranger relationship." Under such arrangements a villager of means provided for the needs of the caravan, and in return the caravan leader would give gifts, on leaving, commensurate with the services rendered.

When large caravans neared the coast, leaders exercised options on how and where to proceed with the sale. Prices offered, goods available, and local political circumstances affected decisions concerning which routes to take or markets to seek. Throughout most years of the trade, slaves from the Muslim network were marched all the way to the Atlantic ports in Senegambia, and they began reaching coastal markets between Guinea and Ivory Coast directly, without sales through middlemen, after 1720.

In the early years Muslim merchants brought slaves to the Gold Coast and the Bight of Benin. However, after the mid-seventeenth century, strong states gained control of trade between European forts on the Gold Coast and the Niger Delta, and another pattern of slave marketing arose there. Early slaving in this region brought new military technology—firearms to the Gold Coast and horses to the Slave Coast—and that technology enabled states to arise. Asante and Oyo were the most powerful and thus are best known, but other states existed at various times and became tributary to or incorporated into the larger entities. These states had the military power to prevent Muslim traders from penetrating their northern limits and to contain Europeans in their coastal outposts. In between, they controlled slave procurement and marketing. They obtained slaves through tribute from conquered territories; they favored their own government traders and restricted foreign and local merchants. For a time one of these states, Dahomey, even limited exchange on its coast to a single trader, the state agent, the "Yovogon" at Whydah.

Throughout the interior of the Bight of Benin, inland marketing centers existed where itinerant merchants met with representatives of outlying chiefs who had acquired slaves in a variety of ways—purchase, capture, tribute payment, or gift. After making sure their own labor supplies were adequate, chiefs exchanged slaves for luxury goods or military equipment (especially horses) that might help them capture more slaves. In larger markets special brokers fed slaves and provided them shelter before the sale. Once the merchants acquired slaves, some marched them directly to the coast, using them as porters to carry leather goods, textiles, foodstuffs, or other items to exchange in local or regional trade. Others moved only a short way before selling their slaves, who then underwent passage through a chain of traders with smaller caravans, generally heading coastward. On the edge of communities lining major routes of slave movement were *zangos*, designated resting places where merchants and their slaves and pack animals could get food and water and find shelter. Once on the coast, merchants exchanged slaves and other trade items for goods to take back into the interior. These included textiles, spirits, tobacco, firearms, and decorative items. The traders sometimes retained some slaves to use as porters on the return.

Farther east and south, inland of the Bight of Biafra where the Ibo and Ibibio lived, a private system of marketing control prevailed. Absence of centralized states did not lessen the ability of traders to produce slaves. The trade from the Bight of Biafra grew greatly after 1730. By mid-century it provided one-third of all the slaves carried in English ships. What developed with the increase in demand were commercial associations that competed for slaves from the interior and for markets at such infamous ports as Bonny, Brass, and Calabar. These associations often were tied to Ibo, Ijaw, Igala, and Aro religious shrines. Over time the Aro won almost complete control of slave procurement and delivery. By the mid-eighteenth century regular Aro markets operated across a series of trading routes in the interior. In some places Aro associations organized mercenary forces to conduct slave raids northward toward the Benue River valley. When European captains came to the Biafran coast they visited port towns near the mouths of the many rivers and extended credit in trade goods to one of the local commercial associations (or "trading houses"). These associations sent armed parties in enormous boats up the rivers to the Aro markets and returned with slaves.

Below Biafra, along the coasts of Congo and Angola, states, including the region of Portuguese control, centered on Luanda, worked to control trade as rigidly as they could, but competition from private African traders made long-term monopoly impossible. Thus prices remained low. Within this structure developed a network of perhaps unequaled efficiency that in the seventeenth and eighteenth centuries was able to deliver for export over 2.5 million slaves.

North of the Zaire were three major harbors (Loango Bay, Malomba, and Cabinda) where, particularly after 1680, masters of English, Dutch, and French ships met with representatives of the Vili kingdom to acquire slaves. Ship captains had to obtain licenses to trade, which allowed them to construct temporary shelters for the Africans they acquired. Royal Vili officials negotiated customs fees and supervised brokers who helped Vili merchants and European buyers agree on prices. From these ports to the interior was a Vili trade diaspora. Rulers organized heavily guarded caravans that ventured to markets several hundred miles away with salt, palm oil, and cloth. Merchants from farther inland brought slaves and ivory for exchange.

In contrast to Vili control of the coast north of the Zaire, Portuguese crown officials dominated slave acquisition and marketing south of the great river. For half a century after 1650, governors and *capitaes mores* based in Luanda exploited and abused the nearby populations. These officials provided recognition to African chiefs and then charged them tribute payments in slaves; they raided more distant African settlements for slaves, hiring their own soldiers for such work in violation of orders from Lisbon; and they granted sanction to private Portuguese raiding parties. Then, around the beginning of the eighteenth century, government-organized slave raiding diminished and private Portuguese, mulatto, and African merchants took over. These traders left Luanda or Benguela with trade goods that commercial firms on the coast advanced them and headed for one of several major interior trading centers. There they exchanged their goods for between a score and one hundred slaves and brought them back to the port for holding. As demand on the coast increased, important slaving markets developed in the near and far interior. In a sense, the system of the coastal region reproduced itself in stages toward the interior, where African states sent their own agents farther inland to markets and fairs that drew slaves from their own hinterlands. By the end of the eighteenth century slaves were coming to the Angola coast from beyond the upper Kasai River, seven hundred miles into the interior.

The variety of marketing systems that existed between Senegambia and Angola affected how European merchants acquired slaves but meant little to the humans who were the products of the systems. The hardships Africans encountered from the time of enslavement to the point of sale reach beyond the limits of the imagination. Mungo Park, the Scottish physician who explored the upper Niger River at the end of the eighteenth century, traveled back to the coast with a Muslim-organized slave caravan. Some of the slaves had been taken in raids and held in irons for three years before sale. Once on the march, Park writes, the slaves

are commonly secured, by putting the right leg of one, and the left of another, into the same pair of fetters. By supporting the fetters with a string, they can walk, very slowly. Every four slaves are likewise fastened together by the necks, with a strong rope of twisted thongs; and in the night, an additional pair of fetters is put on their hands, and sometimes a light iron chain passed round their necks.

Shelter for slaves was normally like that provided the pack animals—a stockaded area of bare ground. Slaves ate cheaply, thus poorly, of whatever the local fare. Corn, millet, or yams were staples, depending on location. What cooking was done the captives did for themselves. The caravans were largely self-contained. On the march to the coast following his capture near his home in Guinea, six-year-old Broteer Furro (who took the name Venture Smith in America) had to carry on his head a twenty-five-pound stone for grinding the caravan's corn.

Another difficult time for slaves was the period of waiting in port. Food was scarce in some seasons and water was seldom abundant. Caravan leaders, buyers, sellers, ship captains—all were eager to skimp on supplies to reduce overhead.

Overlooked for many years were the epidemiological difficulties slaves experienced when marched from one disease environment to another. Africans brought up in the savannas contracted sleeping sickness in the forests; those reared in drier or higher areas caught malaria or yellow fever in the wetter lowlands; and different strains of influenza and other diseases often lurked in regions even closer to their homes. Death rates varied across the slave-trading area and through time; they are impossible to estimate with accuracy. However, Curtin speculates that more slaves died in Africa as they passed among different disease environments than died after reaching the coast or in transit to the New World.

## The Slaving Voyage

By the time English planters began importing slaves directly from Africa into mainland North America, the Atlantic trade had been in operation for over two centuries. Enough word had passed through the shipyards and docks of Bristol and London from experienced traders to make most English captains wise to the business. Within broad parameters they knew where to go along the African coast, what types of trade goods to take, and how to get along under usual conditions. Although they always hoped for good winds and rapid transactions, they knew it would take, on average, two months to reach the farthest slave marts in Angola with stops for water and supplies;

they knew loading was unpredictable but that stopping at different ports over several months to procure slaves and provisions might be necessary; and they figured on another thirty to forty days with decent winds in the Atlantic crossing to North America. They were also aware of other key factors. The healthiest time of year to sail close to Africa's tropical shores north of the equator was during the English winter months, vice versa for lands south of the line. They knew how thoroughly disease could decimate a ship's crew and its human cargo. Finally they knew that the market for slaves in Virginia or South Carolina was greatest (and prices were highest) during the cropping season of late April into early November, when it would also be easiest to get a return cargo of colonial produce. For these reasons, it seemed wise to leave the British isles with designs of landing in the colonies in the early summer. This required planning for different ports of call and was always open to disruption from the vagaries of slave supply, the availability of food and water, proper sailing winds, and more. However, records show how good their planning was. No slave ships from Africa ever entered the Chesapeake in December, January, or February.

By the time English shippers began coming to the North American mainland directly from Africa, they had settled on an optimal size and design for their vessels. Most English slavers after 1680 were of "middling" size, 100–200 tons; the size increased gradually through the eighteenth century. The typical vessel arriving in Virginia or South Carolina straight from Africa carried about 200 slaves. In the earlier days regular merchant ships were employed and carpenters built temporary platforms to hold the human cargo on the Atlantic passage. Later, ships built especially for slaving became the norm. These were long, narrow, fast vessels, built with ports and gratings to direct air below decks. In addition to equipment particular to the voyage—shackling irons and ropes mainly, but also nets to prevent escape when near land—the slave ship had to carry an inordinately large number of casks for food and water. A ship with 404 slaves and a crew of 47 left Africa with 13,000 pounds of food. The English slaver *Brookes* on her voyage with 600 Africans and 45 sailors carried 34,000 gallons of water. And room had to remain to stow firewood for cooking.

Crews on slave ships were larger than normal, about one crew member for every ten slaves, because of the special needs to feed and control the captives. African duty was more dangerous and less popular than any other. Paid little and often crimped or taken from jail for slaving service, the crews were generally a hard lot, victims themselves of the economic system that employed them. Exceptions were the captain, who often had a stake in the slaving venture; the ship's surgeon, whose presence had minimal effect on slave or crew mortality; carpenters and coopers.

Captains usually stuck to one of two modes of trade along the African Coast: ship trade and shore trade. However, most traded both ways depending on the necessities of the location. Good harbors, roadsteads, or river estuaries that appeared relatively free of disease brought buyers to shore. Rough surf, seasonal unhealthiness, or merchants willing to come to the ships to barter led to transactions on board.

Shippers coming south from Europe found they had to deal, sometimes extensively, with local African political authorities. Those who wanted to take advantage of established outposts and of the enterprise of the surrounding communities almost always had to satisfy local African officials with payments of "custom" before trading began. Custom sometimes proved onerous in cost and time. In the Gambia River, where English chartered companies maintained a fort and garrison on James Island, slavers lost time in what today one might call "red tape." Captain Charles Heatly, master of an English vessel trading for slaves in the 1660s, described the procedure:

When a ship arrives in the River Gambia she comes to an anchor at Gillofree Port, in the Kingdom of Barra, opposite James Fort on James' Island. . . . You send your boat on shore to acquaint the Alkaide or Mayor of the town of your arrival; he in common returns with the boat, and receives from you an anchorage-money. Ten gallons of liquor for the king, value 30s., and two iron bars for himself, value 7s., and perhaps presents, a few bottles of wine, beer, cyder, etc. He immediately despatches messengers with the liquor as above to the king, informing him that such vessel is arrived, and only wants to pay his Customs, intending to proceed up the river. The king consults his councillors for a proper day to receive the same, and sends word to the alkaide accordingly. After a detention of four, five, six and seven days, he sends his people to receive his Custom, 140 bars in merchandise, amount sterling on an average £16.

If the fort had slaves on hand, the slaver might procure them and sail on to another location. Seldom did one outpost have enough to fill the holds of even small vessels. The captain could opt to remain at anchor off the outpost on the prospect that more slaves would be coming by caravan from the interior. Intelligence of such activity was surprisingly good. At big markets caravans arrived with regularity. News of the approach of large numbers of slaves traveled fast and far. Commanders at outposts or ship captains could send word inland of demand for slaves on the coast in hopes of luring caravans to their factories. Caravan leaders seemed aware of relative demand and competitive prices.

At times during the trade's heyday, from the 1740s through the rest of the century, competition at slaving markets on the coast grew exceptionally keen. A vessel that sailed to the Loango Coast north of the Congo in 1742 found fourteen other European vessels there, and it took four months to purchase a cargo of 362 slaves. Many ships simply failed to get a full load and crossed the Atlantic with a partial cargo.

Considering everything from the cost of trade goods and transportation to customs duties, broker fees, food costs, and markups by middlemen, slaves were generally a good value for European buyers. Prices in the English market in the Gambia River were typical of those along the coast, rising steadily from the early years of the trade. In the 1680s one healthy adult slave cost an English buyer on average £5.47, but that price rose gradually to £9.43 in the 1720s, £10.05 in the 1740s, £14.10 in the 1760s, and £20.95 in the 1780s. Profit in the enterprise is evident in prices for slaves in the American market. A healthy adult slave in Virginia in 1690 brought £15, in 1760, £45.

At the point of sale the English buyer, sometimes in the company of a surgeon or an experienced hand, examined the available slaves. Parties figured slave values in a standard unit of labor, "one good slave," which was originally one young male slave between eighteen and twenty-five and in good health, but later came to represent women as well as men somewhat older. Slaves below this standard counted as a fraction. With the assistance of a broker, English buyer and African seller bargained until they agreed on a price for the lot of the people for sale. Bargaining was usually in a fictitious currency of the region. They dickered in "bars" (from the original iron bars imported into West Africa) from Senegambia to the Ivory Coast, in "trade ounces" (based on an ounce of gold dust) on the Gold Coast, and in "manilas" (bracelet-like pieces of brass), cowrie shells, and cloth currency elsewhere. The currencies fluctuated, sometimes widely, and separate rates of exchange existed for different African exports, usually depending on the bargain struck by the individuals. But the bargaining was not as simple as the buyer agreeing to provide so much cloth, for example, for so many slaves. African merchants were interested in an *assortment* of goods they could resell, and the shipper with the proper mix of imports in his possession saw the value of each rise accordingly. No English merchant with just a few different commodities to exchange could expect a good deal on slaves. A typical assortment of goods exchanged for 180 Africans in the Gambia River in 1740–41 included 1,178 silver coins, 164 guns, 119 gallons of rum, 1,140 lbs. of gunpowder, 150 pieces of linen, 430 iron bars, 92 cutlasses, 450 gunflints, 66 lbs. of carnelian beads, 2,556 lbs. of salt, 63 pieces of Indian textile, 4,391 lbs. of glass beads, 219 yards of woolen cloth, 35 lbs. of lead balls, 288 lbs. of crystal, 102 brass pans, 662 lbs. of pewterware, 71 pairs of pistols, 37 lbs. of cowrie shells, 30 pieces of Manchester textiles, 398 lbs. of fringe, 47 reams of paper, and 2 copper rods.

The meeting of African captive with English shipper was fraught with trauma for the slave. Notwithstanding the deep shock of initial enslavement and forced removal to the coast, the African now confronted frightening new forces: an alien group of sharp-nosed Europeans occupying the strange construction of a sailing ship, afloat on the saltwater expanse of the unfamiliar Atlantic. Joseph C. Miller (in *Way of Death: Merchant Capitalism and the Angola Slave Trade, 1730–1830*, 1988) describes the experience at port towns along the Angola coast:

All the slaves trembled in terror at meeting the white cannibals of the cities, the first Europeans whom many of the slaves would have seen. They feared the whites' intention of converting Africans' brains into cheese or rending the fat of African bodies into cooking oil, as well as burning their bones into gunpowder. They clearly regarded the towns as places of certain death, as indeed they became for many, if not for the reasons slaves feared.

Olaudah Equiano (in *Interesting Narrative of the Life of Olaudah Equiano, or Gustavus Vassa, the African, written by himself,* 1789, edited by Paul Edwards, 1967), from southern Nigeria, recalled the experience vividly:

The first object which saluted my eyes when I arrived on the coast was the sea, and a slave ship which was then riding at anchor and waiting for its cargo. These filled me with astonishment, which was soon converted into terror when I was carried on board. I was immediately handled and tossed up to see if I were sound by some of the crew, and I was now persuaded that I had gotten into a world of bad spirits and that they were going to kill me. Their complexions too differing so much from ours, their long hair and the language they spoke (which was very different from any I had ever heard) united to confirm me in this belief. Indeed such were the horrors of my views and fears at the moment that, if ten thousand worlds had been my own, I would have freely parted with them all to have exchanged my condition with that of the meanest slave in my own country. When I looked round the ship too and saw a large furnace or copper boiling and a multitude of black people of every description chained together, every one of their countenances expressing dejection and sorrow, I no longer doubted my fate; and quite overpowered with horror and anguish, I fell motionless on the deck and fainted.

It is difficult to assess the psychological effect of the entire experience on the captive because of the lack of evidence, but some witnesses described what one might assume—a continued state of chronic depression was the norm for Africans through much of the time following their enslavement and movement. Surgeons on board slaving vessels noted "a gloomy pensiveness" or "fixed melancholy" on the visages of Africans. As we know now, such mental states probably had adverse effects on their abilities to ward off illness, and in a number of cases their situations prompted men and women to commit suicide.

Not all slaves boarded a vessel at once. A person sent aboard just prior to departure for the Americas might be joining others who had been on the ship for a matter of weeks or months. The treatment the Africans received at initial boarding did not lessen their sense of trauma. Some masters had crews wash down and shave slaves, ostensibly for reasons of health. Shackles were common for all while close to shore and for adult men even longer. Experienced captains girded their vessels with nets to prevent escapes overboard.

Assessing the voyage from the African coast to ports in British North America, the so-called middle passage, is difficult to do in a fair, accurate way. No more than a handful of Africans who experienced the trip left records, and those who did were not altogether typical. Some wrote their accounts in an effort to end the slave trade. Englishmen who left written accounts of their experiences as masters or crewmen on slavers, or who testified before parliamentary committees investigating the traffic, usually did so for a reason. Some wanted to justify slaving, so they likely underplayed the horrors of life on board ship; others wanted to have Parliament outlaw the African trade, so they amassed evidence and emphasized the worst parts of the slaving voyage. When considering the raw inhumanity of the whole episode, it is not easy to examine the middle passage and weigh its effects dispassionately, but recent studies that focus on statistical evaluation of the thousands of voyages aid one's attempt to do so. These studies show that efforts toward more or less humane treatment of the captives mattered little in the way they coped with the voyage. Random influences, or at least factors largely beyond the control of even the most experienced and skillful captains, had the greatest effect on slave health and mortality between Africa and the Americas.

In demographic terms, the typical shipload composition of captive Africans coming to the British American mainland was not drastically different from the makeup of other ships transporting Europeans to the New World. Two times as many African men as women crossed the Atlantic; fewer than one in ten slaves transported was under ten years old. Students of the trade long thought the larger number of adult men was a result of planter preferences in the Americas, but new studies suggest that supply factors did more to dictate the composition of the cargo. The demand for women was high in the colonies, for they did most of the same work as men; prices for men and women were not always the same, but often they were close. However, the Africans controlling who entered the slave trade were apt to retain women slaves, whom they valued more highly—as agricultural producers primarily, but also as bearers of offspring—than men. Young children were simply less economical to trade. They cost as much to enslave and transport, yet they brought lower prices.

Basic elements of the voyage are easy to establish. Africans had little room below decks. They were not all stowed as spoons set in a drawer, as depicted in the widely published plan of the *Brookes*. It is a diagram of a particularly bad case, with men and women barely having headroom to sit upright. Many slavers did not plan to load slaves so densely and many did not take on as many slaves as planned. Nevertheless, on average, slaves had less than half the space accorded contemporary European shipboard convicts (like those who made the voyage to Australia), emigrants (like those indentured servants settling the same English mainland colonies), or soldiers (like those hauled over to fight in the American Revolution). Slave decks were usually four or five feet high, but sometimes they were lower. Captains kept Africans topside through much of the day as weather permitted. It was better for the people and it enabled crews to go below and make feeble efforts to swab out. Men remained connected to one another with leg irons that were fastened to chains running along the deck. In spite of such fettering, crews encouraged movement and activity.

Ideas of hygiene on shipboard were primitive. Captains made a reasonable effort to guard food and water from contamination and to isolate the sickest slaves, but sanitary facilities were inadequate under the best of conditions, and bilges grew foul in a hurry. The worst times were when bad weather forced people below for long periods. Grates and canvas airfoils admitted insufficient fresh air. A ship becalmed meant bad conditions for all. Below decks it could get murderously hot and downright fetid. Alexander Falconbridge, who served as surgeon on slave ships (and who in 1788 wrote *An Account of the Slave Trade on the Coast of Africa* to acquaint the English public with the abuses of the trade), tells of one such occasion:

Some wet and blowing weather having occasioned port-holes to be shut and the grating to be covered, fluxes and fevers among the negroes ensued. While they were in this situation, I frequently went down among them till at length their rooms became so extremely hot as to be only bearable for a very short time. But the excessive heat was not the only thing that rendered their situation intolerable. The deck, that is, the floor of their rooms, was so covered with the blood and mucus which had proceeded from them in consequence of the flux, that it resembled a slaughter-house.

Whether one could smell a slaver before sighting it, as was often said, depended on wind speed and direction, but the very idea suggests the unpleasant and unhealthy conditions for the persons on board.

Captains normally purchased food for the crossing on the African coast. What the slaves ate depended in part on where they left Africa. Corn and rice were staples for vessels leaving the less-forested coasts (Senegambia, Angola). Yams were standard fare from the Niger Delta to the Zaire River. English captains who brought provisions from home carried dried beans for their ease of storage and general acceptance. "Three meals a day" is a modern convention that concerned slavers little. Slaves normally ate twice, morning and evening, in small groups out of communal tubs. Each one received about a pint of water with a meal.

It is not clear to what extent the density of slaves on board—whether shipmasters packed people in loosely (in relative terms) or tightly—affected mortality. In his *Way of Death* Miller argues that "tight packing" meant heavier mortality on Portuguese slavers plying the trade between Angola and Brazil. However, studies of the English trade show that as the tendency of slavers to raise the number of captives on board grew through the eighteenth century, mortality rates generally declined. What affected mortality more than anything else may have been the simple factor of time at sea. This varied according to the length of the voyage (Senegambia to Virginia is just over four thousand miles; Angola to Virginia nearly six thousand) and the ship's speed, which existing winds dictated. Most captains planned for a voyage of from forty to sixty days. Longer voyages had higher rates of mortality, mainly because of contamination of food and water that brought on dysentery, the dreaded "flux" that was the biggest killer.

Still another important factor in mortality on the voyage was a slave's region of origin in Africa. Persons from Angola and the Bight of Benin seem to have had the highest mortality rate. Those from the Loango Coast, in between, died less often. Why this was the case is puzzling, but the individual's health at embarkation seems to have been most important. Such uncontrollable factors as the length of the march to the port, regional drought or famine, or strength of demand on the coast (prompting Africans to sell weaker persons when demand drove prices higher) affected health and, consequently, mortality on the voyage.

Mortality rates in the middle passage were, on average, in the neighborhood of 16 percent. This was close to the death rates of prisoners and soldiers on ocean voyages until the second half of the eighteenth century, when all mortality rates dropped—but those of slaves less so. The 16-percent figure is misleading for consideration of the typical slaving voyage, for most slavers crossing the Atlantic had a lower mortality rate. Captains wanted it so. If they were paid according to the profit of the voyage, which was tied to sales, they strove to keep slave deaths at a minimum. The average is skewed upwards by a small number of vessels that experienced astronomical mortality, almost always because of an uncontrollable epidemic of measles or smallpox on board. It is skewed, too, by the results of perils at sea that were common to all at the time: shipwrecks, sinkings, pirate attacks. Shipboard slave revolts occurred occasionally and resulted in loss of life, but they were not a frequent happening. Among Rhode Island slavers, between 1730 and 1807, there was one revolt for every fifty-five vessels, or one during every four and one-half years of slaving. Middle-passage mortality was heavier in the earlier days of the trade. After 1750 mortality rates in the passage declined noticeably. Reasons for this are several. The speed of ships increased with new designs and such innovations as copper sheathing, thus cutting the important element of time at sea. Also, after the 1760s captains learned that they could prevent scurvy by feeding people citrus fruits, and they learned then, too, that fresh water could be produced by boiling and evaporating salt water.

Dangers of the voyage were not over with landfall. Africans who had become inured to a host of diseases endemic to their tropical homes were again in an environment with new diseases, new foods, and different water. Some ports required several weeks quarantine of arriving vessels, and it took days or weeks to arrange for sale. This was always a time of further slave mortality. In colonial Virginia between 1710 and 1718, for example, over 5 percent of the captive Africans died between the time they reached America and their sale.

The sale of slaves worked differently in various colonial ports. In the Chesapeake the experience of the *John and Betty* with "King" Carter was typical. Large slaveowners in the region were the central figures in most economic dealings; buying and selling slaves was no exception. Captains of vessels entering the Chesapeake with lists of prominent planters who might serve as middlemen, cast around for the best deal. Commissions of 7 or 8 percent were common. The planters evaluated buyers' credit, helped obtain return cargoes, arranged for provisions, and sometimes made deals for leasing slaves. They carried out transactions on shipboard where the Africans remained quartered.

By the mid-eighteenth century methods of selling slaves in the colonies had become regular, or in some places even institutional. Charleston (with its smaller neighboring ports of Georgetown and Beaufort) was the major port of entry on the British colonial mainland, importing one-quarter of all slaves brought into the mainland colonies through 1775. Savannah had slave dealings from the 1760s, and Philadelphia and New York imported slaves on a smaller scale. In many ports wealthy planters had an interest in merchant firms, and regular slavers established relations with one of these firms for slave marketing. Eighteen such firms did 60 percent of the slaving business in Charleston. Individual merchant houses might at one time have a consignment of several hundred slaves to sell. They did the advertising and most often sold the slaves at public auction for cash or commodities. Some provided credit for needy buyers. If the market was not promising, the firm might hold the Africans until prospects improved, but the costs of food and shelter had to be weighed in the decision.

From one of the main points of entry, slaves were transported across an increasingly wide part of the colonies' southern Atlantic hinterland. From Charleston, large numbers of slaves moved on into Georgia after about 1750, smaller numbers went to North Carolina, and coasting vessels moved slaves northward to other British mainland colonies.

Arrival on a plantation or a small farm in America meant part of a test for the Africans was completed. Being alive was a victory of sorts. From the time of enslavement in Africa, through passage to the coast, across the Atlantic, and to a location of some permanence in America, more than one-third of all the victimized Africans died. Now they had to add one more task to survival—to acculturate and learn to get by in a new land under radically different circumstances. Above all, the newcomers to America had to learn to perform their new work as their owners directed, for the vast Atlantic slaving system brought them to the colonies as a commodity of labor. This fact would play the biggest role in directing the lives of the slaves and their offspring in the new land for generations to come.

# CHAPTER TWO

# Development of Slavery in English North America

When the first English colonists settled Jamestown in 1607, they did not have in mind establishing an economy and society based on slavery. None of the earliest settlers of colonial Virginia and Maryland intended specifically to import African chattel slaves for their work force. But black slavery appeared in these colonies before the middle of the seventeenth century, and it grew rapidly after 1680. By a little after 1700, over half of all the laborers in the two Chesapeake colonies were of African origin and enslaved.

The institution of black slavery began slowly in Virginia and Maryland; it caught on there and in some other new mainland colonies as the seventeenth century ran its course. In a narrow sense, it began because colonists with bountiful land were having difficulty finding an adequate, stable labor force to make their efforts, mostly at growing tobacco, pay. White servitude worked for some decades alongside black slavery, but the latter soon proved more economical and fraught with fewer problems for the landowners. But, in a larger sense, black slavery began in the English mainland colonies without much questioning, perhaps inevitably, because the colonies were part of the growing Atlantic colonial economic system that produced staples for the European market and relied on the labor that best fit its needs. In the Atlantic world of the mid-seventeenth century, African chattel slavery was a recognized and increasingly preferred labor supply. Throughout tropical parts of the New World from Brazil to Cuba, black slavery was spreading rapidly. Planters could work Africans harder and control them more thoroughly than they could European servants, and because Africans were inexpensive by comparison with other laborers, they brought owners greater profits. So British colonists in Virginia and Maryland were not trying something radically different when, after 1680, they began buying large numbers of Africans to work their lands. They were following what by then had become a conventional pattern in the Atlantic colonial system.

English settlers came to the mainland colonies to prosper, and the way to do so was tied to trade. Each colony was to find something to produce for the home market and then, with a favorable balance of trade, purchase imports made in England. The main variation among the colonies was in items produced. Virginia and Maryland grew tobacco at first, and then over time they diversified and began producing cereals and livestock for export primarily to other English colonies. Low-country South Carolina and Georgia moved in the other direction, exporting livestock and timber before establishing plantations for growing rice and indigo. Northern colonies produced food, including fish, and all the colonies, but especially the northern ones, participated in a carrying trade. In every sense, producing for export fueled a need for laborers. The commodities produced would be the most important determinant of the size and type of labor force that the English colonists would require.

Of course, the mainland colonies did not exist alone in these enterprises. They had close ties to English islands in the Caribbean. English shipping serviced both areas. Islanders emigrated to the mainland when opportunities seemed greater. Mainland colonists knew well what was taking place in the rest of the Atlantic world but were especially attuned to the English Caribbean. Beginning in the 1640s, Barbados planters made the change from tobacco and cotton production to sugarcane, and as they did so they opted for African slave labor over the white servants they had been using. Jamaica and the other English Leeward Islands (Antigua, Monteserrat, Nevis, and St. Christopher) followed suit. By the last quarter of the seventeenth century the plantation model, with owners using repressive force to get extraordinary amounts of work out of African men and women held in bondage, existed "next door" to the mainland colonies. It is not surprising that the mainland colonies began to import African slaves in large numbers. What seems more surprising is that they waited so long to begin doing so.

When examining the development of slavery in the mainland colonies, it is important to bear in mind what Ira Berlin emphasizes in "Time, Space, and the Evolution of Afro-American Society in British Mainland North America," *American Historical Review*, 80 (1980). Black slavery came into being at different times in various mainland regions; it began for different reasons (though some factors were similar); and through the seventeenth and eighteenth centuries various forms of slave systems developed in different mainland areas. Berlin recognizes three such systems: one in the Chesapeake region with smaller plantations; one in the Carolina and Georgia low country with larger plantations; and one in the northern colonies without plantations at all. These separate regions had different economies and particular labor needs; so over the years they developed different demographic characteristics, especially in the proportion of blacks to whites and native-born Africans to persons of African descent born in the colonies (commonly referred to as creoles). This interplay of factors determined the nature of the slave system and the African American society that evolved in each of the regions.

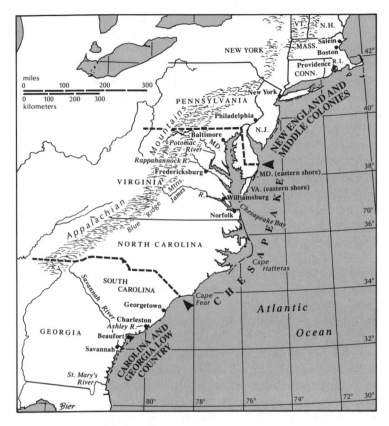

The English Colonies of the North American Mainland
in the Eighteenth Century

## The Chesapeake

The first English settlers in colonial Virginia (after 1607) and
Maryland (after 1634) found a temperate climate and land that
was abundant, fertile, and thinly populated. "The mildnesse
of the aire, the fertilitie of the soile, and the situation of the
rivers," wrote John Smith in *A Map of Virginia* (1612), "are

so propitious to the nature and use of man as no place is more convenient for pleasure, profit, and man's sustenance." It was a land "overgrowne with trees" that, in Smith's vision, could "soone be amended by good husbandry." This seemed ideal for what the merchants and speculators who paid for the colonial venture wanted: rapid profits. They hoped settlers could quickly begin producing a staple crop not grown in England, sell it on the English market, and buy English manufactures in return. This early enterprise would prompt more Englishmen to come to the colonies and grow more of the staple; taxes on the exchange would help the crown; and the fields of the American mainland would be places to send the alarming number of landless, often unemployed Englishmen who were posing a threat to a society that suffered from declining real wages, civil war, and social turmoil.

If Virginia and Maryland did not fit the model exactly as the original financiers had dreamed of it, the two colonies came close. Within a decade of settlement Virginia colonists were growing tobacco, which the English used more than any other Europeans, and getting good prices for its export while importing a variety of English-made commodities. There was land for the claiming—so long as colonists could control the Native Americans who lived on it—and opportunity seemed boundless. As tobacco boomed there grew a demand for laborers probably beyond the expectations of the early colonial planters. Still, England had plenty of poor men wanting work, so it was primarily these young men (median age sixteen) who came to the colonies in the early decades to work the tobacco fields. Unable to afford their own passage, the laborers made arrangements with recruiters in English market centers to repay their fare through work in the new lands. Thus, they came mostly as servants—some as tenants working for shares of their crop, some as bond servants, some as apprentices. All had fairly long (five to seven years) terms of servitude.

Early colonial planters were not tied solely to English servants, however. For a time there was hope that Native Americans would work in the fields, benefit from "English civilizing tendencies," and develop a harmonious relationship with the colonists. This vision never panned out for a variety of reasons, but largely, it seems, because the Native Americans' lifestyle was not that of a regimented cultivator. They balked at the work and ran off or died under the strain.

English mainland colonists imported persons of African descent too, the first in Jamestown in 1619, and they seemed to fit the colonial ideal better. Although what their precise status was is not clear, these early African arrivals were servants in somewhat the same sense as their white counterparts. Most were probably closer to slaves than to indentured servants. On the whole they seemed to serve longer than whites. Still, they were far from being like the chattel slaves of the tidewater plantations a century later. By most accounts their lives were not significantly different from those of English servants in the same place at the same time. Some Africans in Virginia gained their freedom; some owned servants themselves. T. H. Breen and Stephen Innes in a fascinating little book, *'Myne Owne Ground': Race and Freedom on Virginia's Eastern Shore, 1640–1676*, (1980), found that in Virginia's Northampton County there was a time around the middle of the seventeenth century when a number of resourceful blacks purchased their freedom and entered into the class of small planters. "They became part of a complex human network," the authors conclude, "and it was their success in dealing with white planters, great and small, servants and slaves, that in large measure explains their viability." Stories of some of these free blacks stand out in the records. One Virginia arrival, identified only as "Antonio a Negro" and sold as something approximating a slave in 1621, survived an Indian assault with four others (out of the fifty-six men on their plantation), married an African woman, and by 1650, as Anthony Johnson, had acquired his freedom along with 250 acres and a herd of cattle. Five years later, on advice from his extended family, Johnson successfully sued a white man, Robert Parker, for detaining a slave belonging to Johnson. The Johnson clan moved to Somerset, Maryland, in the 1660s, where they continued to prosper, in a fashion, until the turn of the century. Another free African American, Francis Payne, worked six years to be able to purchase two servants and 1,650 pounds of tobacco with which he bought his freedom. He then worked seven more years for wages and acquired 3,800 pounds of tobacco, enough to buy his wife and children from slavery. And Johnson and Payne were not alone. In Northampton County between 1664 and 1677, ten of fifty-three black males were free householders. These free blacks lived like the whites who were not of the wealthiest class. They owned land, grew crops, raised livestock, traded, argued in the courts, and had broad social relationships, some legal and moral and some not. But the number of blacks, free or serving, remained small through mid-century. Out of a Chesapeake population of nearly thirteen thousand, only three hundred were of African descent.

With some exceptions, the early experience of white and black servants in the American colonies was neither a pleasant nor rewarding one. Most wanted to come to the colonies, complete their periods of service, work a few years for wages, and then obtain land, acquire their own servants, and gradually enter the wealthier, planter class. Some were able to achieve their goal. Many did not. Servitude was not what they expected, not at all like servitude in England. In order to make the most of the tobacco boom, planters extracted from their servants all the labor they could, and this was far more work than young Englishmen were used to doing. As a consequence, discipline grew harsh and servants soon became, in the eyes of those who worked them, less human and more a commodity. If their status was better than that of African slaves on the larger sugar plantations on Caribbean islands at the same time, the difference was not marked. Furthermore, and no doubt more importantly for those involved, not many servants lived long enough to become planters on any scale. Because of typhoid, malaria, influenza, measles, and smallpox, for most who came to the British mainland colonies during the first third of the century, the new land was a deathtrap.

Immigrants to the mainland began living longer after the 1640s, though, and for a time opportunity was abundant. However, for several decades tobacco prices had been falling and wages remained low. Large planters and speculators had obtained much of the good tidewater land. Edmund S. Morgan in *American Slavery, American Freedom: The Ordeal of Colonial Virginia* (1975) describes the consequences for Chesapeake laborers. Growing numbers of young men who lived through their indentures were unable to acquire the resources to buy land. Soon there developed a group of young men similar to those feared in England—poor, landless, restless vagabonds living on the margins of wealthier society. Such men were especially dangerous in the colonies where all men, for their own protection, were armed. They posed a threat to colonial authorities because they resented and envied the ruling landed gentry. Rebellion was in the air, and it became manifest on several occasions—the best known being Bacon's Rebellion in 1676. Landowners tried several methods of preventing the growth of these poorer white classes, including lengthening terms of servitude. They also saw to the passage of laws preventing the propertyless from voting. Still, the problem remained. White servitude had provided a labor force, but it had brought with it a disruptive class of young men, hard to control, similar to the mother country's. By the end of the 1670s some prosperous tidewater landowners involved in governing Virginia and Maryland might have recognized that another form of servitude could give them more complete control for a longer time.

It was not planter fears of rebellious former servants that cut importation of English bondsmen into the Chesapeake, however. It was a combination of declining numbers of young Englishmen willing to venture across the Atlantic, waning opportunity for such men in Virginia and Maryland, and competition from other new colonies for the limited supply of white laborers. Dropping birthrates in England from the 1630s on, coupled with rising real wages for workers in the mother country meant fewer unemployed and footloose men ready to listen to colonial recruiters. Opportunities in the Chesapeake no longer tempted white servants so much after 1680, either, when a long depression in at least a portion of the tobacco market began and made it still more difficult for poor immigrants to acquire enough money to obtain their own land and labor force. Also, opportunity appeared to be greater in New York (taken over from the Dutch in 1664) and Pennsylvania (established in 1681). So the numbers of white bondsmen entering Virginia and Maryland dwindled rapidly. Through the 1690s more whites left the Chesapeake colonies than entered, and white servant immigration was almost completely done with by 1700.

That Chesapeake planters continued to prefer white servants to black slaves is evident through their labor-seeking activities. When they could not acquire enough young Englishmen, they sought young Englishwomen, then young Irishmen. Still, there were not enough whites available, even at the higher prices planters were willing to pay. So out of necessity, it seems, they made the same switch to African slaves that their counterparts on sugar plantations in the Caribbean had done almost half a century earlier.

It was good fortune for the planters that large numbers of English shippers had begun to participate in the carrying trade of slaves from Africa in the last third of the seventeenth century. When the source of white servants dwindled, another cheap, abundant supply of workers was there, these black, from Africa, and bound for life. They may have been "outlandish," unfamiliar with the English language and English ways, but they were comparatively inexpensive and with sufficient force could be made to work hard in the tobacco fields, just like the white servants who preceded them.

The transition to black slavery occurred at a varied pace throughout the Tidewater. The wealthy growers of sweet-scented tobacco in York County, low on the west side of the Chesapeake Bay, bought Africans early. By the 1680s four of every five unfree laborers there were black. Areas farther north made the switch more slowly. By 1695, however, the rush to buy Africans was on; by 1700, Chesapeake planters purchased three thousand Africans, about the same number they had purchased over the previous twenty years. Population figures provide evidence for the switch. In 1660 there were not seventeen hundred blacks in all of Virginia and Maryland, and in 1680 there were still only about forty-six hundred. But by the end of the century the black population of the two colonies had tripled to almost thirteen thousand, and nearly all of them were slaves. Free whites still made up the majority of tobacco laborers in 1700, but black slaves had become the laborers of choice, and slave labor was rapidly gaining ground on free labor.

Once the institution of black slavery was established, demand took over and pulled slave vessels crossing the ocean from Africa. From 1700 the Atlantic trade would be the major source of labor until the slave population could sustain natural growth, and that would be awhile. Mortality rates for "unseasoned" slaves in English North America remained high through the first two decades of the eighteenth century. Also, from Africa came an imbalance of men, which automatically meant fewer offspring than in a sexually balanced population. Then, too, planters who knew they could obtain young male laborers cheaply through the trade saw no need to import women, and they did not encourage (and probably actively discouraged) childbirth, which hindered a woman's ability to work. So the number of slaves imported annually into the Chesapeake region rose steadily to a peak in about 1740. It was around then that the native-born African American population achieved a rough sexual balance and began to grow naturally. Once the sexual balance evened out, African Americans showed they could indeed be, as some planters considered them, "a prolifick pcople." Darrett and Anita Rutman in *A Place in Time: Middlesex County, Virginia, 1650–1750* (1984) write of one "Sharlott," a twelve-year-old girl purchased by Henry Thacker in 1720. Over forty-four years Sharlott had thirteen children of her own, and in 1764 she, her surviving children, and her grandchildren numbered twenty-two persons—all still Thacker's slaves.

The Atlantic trade into the Chesapeake leveled off and then began a gradual decline toward the last third of the century. But the overall numbers remain startling. Between 1690 and 1770, Chesapeake planters bought about one hundred thousand slaves off vessels from western Africa. On the eve of the American Revolution the nearly two hundred thousand men and women of African descent living around the Chesapeake made up between two-thirds and three-fourths of all Virginia and Maryland's laborers, and they constituted practically the entirety of the agricultural work force.

The growth of black slavery to fill colonial labor needs necessitated a legal basis for the institution. Long-standing precedent was not relevant because English common law did not allow slavery. In fact, more than almost anywhere, individual rights were the basis for much of the law in England. Nevertheless, the economic and social pressures of English planters to create slavery so they could compete successfully with their New World neighbors from Portugal, The Netherlands, and France led to the legal establishment of such an institution in the Americas. Fortunately for mainland planters, English landowners in the Caribbean had worked through the legal difficulties a generation before slavery became an issue in the Chesapeake. Virginia burgesses and Maryland assemblymen could look to Barbados and Jamaica for legal precedent when constructing their own slave codes.

There was a direct relationship between the changing proportion of blacks to whites in a colony and the sense of need a colonial government felt to develop laws regulating the slave population. Tidewater legislators had not bothered to codify slavery until the numbers of slaves swelled and problems with their control arose. Before this time, at least some blacks and whites shared escapades and punishments. In 1649, for instance, William Watts, a white man, and Mary, a black servant, performed the same penance for fornication as any white couple: They had to stand before the congregation in church at Elizabeth River in Virginia, dressed in a white sheet and holding a white wand. But beginning around the middle of the seventeenth century, colonial judges and lawmakers started stripping away the rights of African immigrants. When the erosion of blacks' legal status took place differs by location. In some places courts were treating individual blacks differently from whites by 1640, as indicated by runaway black servant John Punch's sentence "to serve his said master or his assigns for the time of his natural life here or elsewhere." The two white servants who ran away with Punch, "one called Victor, a dutchman, the other a Scotchman called James Gregory," decreed the Virginia court that appeared so careful to record whites' national origins, had to serve their masters an additional year and the colony three years. No white servant in America ever received such a sentence as that of John Punch.

In other places blacks like Anthony Johnson held their own in court cases against whites through the 1660s. But the trend was toward the loss of black rights. In the 1640s blacks in Maryland lost the right to bear firearms. In the 1640s (Virginia) and 1660s (Maryland) black women were included in lists of tithables (because those taxed were "all those that worked in the ground," and black women did so, along with white and black men). In the 1660s both colonies meted out stiff punishment for fornication between individuals of the two races. (Maryland decreed in 1664 that all "English women forgettfull of their free Condicon and to the disgrace of our Nation do intermarry with Negro Slaves . . . shall Serve the master of such slaves during the life of her husband.") Recognizing that masters must make slaves fear for their lives— rather than for the loss of their liberty—to get necessary work from them, and recognizing this required a level of brutality that could result in the slaves' death, Virginia in 1669 passed *"An act about the casual killing of slaves"*:

Be it enacted and declared by this grand assembly, if any slave resist his master (or other by his masters order correcting him) and by the extremity of the correction should chance to die, that his death shall

not be accompted Felony, but the master (or that other person ap-
pointed by the master to punish him) be acquit from molestation,
since it cannot be prepensed malice (which alone makes murther
Felony) should induce any man to destroy his own estate.

Social practice did not always follow the law, so some free
blacks continued to be viable and respected members of Chesapeake communities and had relations with whites on all levels
into the 1670s. But whatever dike held back the flood of legislation and social practice condemning blacks to slavery and
ostracism broke with the importation of large numbers of African slaves after the 1680s. In short order, blacks in the Chesapeake lost most of their remaining rights and found themselves completely set apart from whites on all levels of colonial
society.

The most important loss to the hopes slaves harbored to
attain freedom and any social position was the right to hold
property. For everyone in colonial America, property was the
basis for freedom and dreams of prosperity. In property all
persons had legal rights that gave them confidence in their
dealings with others. In property all persons had self-respect
that manifested itself in a variety of ways favorable to the
individual. Removing African Americans' right to own property took away their ability to accumulate wealth and to participate in the quest for betterment that had once included
almost all mainland colonists. The loss of their right to personal property undermined the possibility for blacks to have
success in personal relations.

Thus, after the first two decades of the eighteenth century,
the Chesapeake colonies were well on their way to becoming
slave societies. The economic and social system that existed
is sometimes characterized in relative terms as one of "smaller
plantations," but that seems to refer to the most evident institutions of the Tidewater and does not describe appropriately
the variety of circumstances in which African Americans lived
at different times and in different places. Until black slavery
caught hold, persons of African descent who lived in the Chesapeake were scattered broadly among white servants and free-

men. Their public contacts were with as many whites as blacks. There was little segregation based on race. African Americans seldom lived on farms with more than a dozen workers of any kind, and only a few lived with more than a handful of other slaves.

With the increase of slavery after 1700, Chesapeake society grew in a direction of having three broad levels based on land and slave holdings. Most landowners lived on family farms of a relatively small size. In Virginia the more prosperous of these might have owned a slave or two or a hired hand, but family members did most of the work. In Maryland by far the largest group of landowners owned no servants or slaves. There also was a middle level of landowners, those with aspirations of becoming big-time planters, who owned a few slaves. These people normally succeeded in joining the class of big planters, or else overextended themselves and failed. The middling farmers were thus a group that was economically and socially "transient," and its numbers declined as the century progressed.

The class of landowners that remained relatively small was that of the largest planters, who owned nearly all of the African Americans in the two colonies. Gloria L. Main in *Tobacco Colony: Life in Early Maryland, 1650–1720* (1982) searched probate records from six Maryland counties and found that through the period of her study two-thirds of all slaves worked for just 6 percent of the planters. On the largest plantations owners hired overseers from the group of young, landless white men who were about, and they drove their workers in gangs and practiced harsh discipline.

The farms, crops, and slaves fell into distinct spatial arrangements. The largest plantations were the tobacco-growing holdings along the Chesapeake Bay and its rivers and inlets. This region formed a tobacco core in the two colonies, with wealth and slaves concentrated on large estates. Around the periphery—the Virginia and Maryland eastern shores, northern Maryland, and areas of Virginia more distant from the water— grain farming and livestock raising were the basic economic activities. Here smaller holdings and fewer slaves were the norm.

Even on large plantations slaves did not always live together in a single group of communal quarters. Instead, planters often housed their slaves in small clusters around their holdings to disperse cattle and hogs, which slaves tended, and to put laborers close to the fields they worked. In Maryland a typical cluster included four or five fieldhands and one or two women to cook, wash, and care for children. Such a cluster might have thirty cattle and twenty hogs to look after and several fields of tobacco to maintain. One of the wealthiest Maryland colonists in 1681, Colonel Benjamin Rozer, owned a work force of sixty-nine slaves and servants. Of these he kept fourteen at the "dwelling plantation" on Port Tobacco Creek, and he settled the others among half a dozen work sites with such names as "Jack's," "Indian Field," and "War Captain's Neck."

Over about a century the establishment and development of black slavery altered nearly every facet of society in the Chesapeake colonies. In 1680 persons of African descent had constituted just a little over 7 percent of the total population of Virginia and Maryland. A century later blacks made up nearly 40 percent of all the people in the two colonies. As the slave population grew, Virginia legislators stayed busy creating new ways of controlling unruly African Americans in their midst. Punishments grew harsh. Philip J. Schwarz in *Twice Condemned: Slaves and the Criminal Laws of Virginia, 1705–1865* (1988) relates the story of Jacob, a slave of Martha Flint of Lancaster County, Virginia, who stood trial with his owner and another white woman for stealing tobacco and food from several local whites. The white women received whippings. Jacob, who could have been hanged for his actions, was granted "mercy" because he acted in the company of "Christian white persons," including the person who owned him. So instead of execution for stealing what turned out to be six pence worth of goods, Jacob was made to stand for an hour at the pillory, to have each ear nailed to the pillory and then cut off "close to the head," and then to receive a "full whipping."

With the growth of black slavery also came about the almost total disappearance of free blacks among the population, a fact that would have considerable effect on the evolution of African American culture in the colonies. By the onset of the Revolution, free blacks made up less than 5 percent of the total Virginia and Maryland black population. A century after slavery had become the preferred institution for colonial labor, persons of African descent lived in considerable numbers throughout the Chesapeake; practically all of them were slaves.

## Carolina and Georgia Low Country

Initial English settlement of the coastal lowland area that stretched from Cape Fear in the north to the St. Mary's River in the south—the area that would be the Atlantic littoral of colonial South Carolina and Georgia—was different in several ways from settlement of the Chesapeake. Early migrants to the area came from other English colonies, Barbados especially in the beginning, as opposed to the British Isles. Like their northern neighbors, they came intent on producing for an English market, but not tobacco. For the first thirty years of settlement they concentrated on providing livestock and timber for the English in the Caribbean and deerskins for those "back home" in England. After that they turned gradually, but then almost totally, to rice production.

The first migrants to South Carolina came after 1670 with a clear sense of who would do the work of production. African slavery had been thriving in the sugarcane fields of Barbados since the 1640s. Two proprietors of South Carolina had been successful Barbadian planters and several others were directors of the Royal African Company, which made its profit off the delivery of slaves to the Americas. The first settlers acquiring low-country land noted "the aptnes of Negroes and other servants fitt for such labor as wilbe there required." So black slaves were present in South Carolina in the year of the colony's founding, and after a generation of settlement persons of African descent constituted a majority of the low-country population. The extension of settlement and agricultural production along the Atlantic low country, then, would mean the spread of an economy and society based on slavery, no matter what else founders and settlers had in mind.

Another important difference between the low country and the Chesapeake had to do with environment. The lowland region was subtropical, a land of summer heat and humidity, swamps and forests. It was more like the islands of the British West Indies or the homelands of many Africans than any part of the British Isles or the northern mainland colonies. Adult slaves who had acquired in Africa some resistance to malaria or yellow fever had advantages over their masters in staying healthy, and they had the benefit of knowing more about subtropical plants and animals and how to work the land. This meant that for the early years of low-country settlement, English masters were more dependent on their slaves than was normally the case. It meant also that Africans would be important in bringing their know-how to bear on developing the colonial low country and particularly on introducing techniques of stock raising and rice production that would help planters find exports for the colonial market.

From its birth as a colony in 1670 through the first thirty years of its existence, South Carolina was a child of Barbados. Its first settlers were from Barbados, its economy was geared to supply Barbados with provisions, and the model life-style of South Carolina landowners was that of Barbadian planters. By 1650 the English island in the Caribbean was seriously overcrowded and most of its arable land was under cultivation. Freed servants lacked opportunity and the population needed provisions. So in the last third of the century there was considerable migration from Barbados to other English colonies in the New World. In 1670 a mix of wealthy planters, freed servants, and slaves of African descent left the island to settle on the Ashley River near what is now Charleston. Quickly they began to produce foods, raise livestock, and harvest timber for the island market.

Whether or not slavery was to be part of South Carolina's economy and society was never a question. Proprietors granted generous amounts of land for bringing black slaves to the colony: "To the Owner of every Negro-Man or Slave, brought thither to settle within the first year, twenty acres; and for every Woman-Negro or Slave, ten acres of Land; and all Men-Negro's or slaves after that time, and within the first five years, ten acres, and for every Woman Negro or slave, five acres." The 1669 Fundamental Constitutions of Carolina, meant to guide the colonists in their new settlement, accepted slavery as a way of life. It was unequivocal in stating, "Every Freeman of Carolina shall have absolute power and authority over Negro slaves of what opinion or Religion soever."

Through its early years, between one-fourth and one-third of the individuals coming to South Carolina were black slaves, predominantly men. Their importance to colonial enterprise was considerable. Some West Africans were experienced breeders and keepers of cattle. English settlers, who picked up some techniques for keeping livestock in subtropical conditions from practices in the Spanish and British West Indies, relied also on African expertise to develop herds. Methods of tending cattle in South Carolina's free-grazing environment tended to combine techniques of husbandry used across West Africa's savannas, which included seasonal burning to freshen grasses and nighttime penning of cattle for protection, with those in use in the Caribbean. The exceptional knowledge of stock raising of peoples along the Gambia River (especially the Fulbe), coupled with the importance of producing livestock for the Barbados market in the early years of South Carolina's struggle to establish itself as a viable colony, helps explain Carolina planters' long-standing preference for Gambian slaves. But if some Africans' experience with animals was useful for a generation of South Carolina's history, others' knowledge of planting and growing a grain crop helped alter the colony's way of life dramatically after 1700. The beginning of rice production brought about a demand for labor that would cause South Carolina to import more slaves than any other mainland colony through the rest of the eighteenth century.

South Carolina settlers went through the same search for a staple that Virginia colonists did in the first decades of the seventeenth century. They performed systematic experiments with a variety of products—cotton, silk, tobacco, indigo, sugarcane, naval stores, ginger, and wine. They experimented with rice also, but through the mid-1690s they did not have much to show for their effort. Then, sometime near the end of the century, Carolinians began to succeed in growing and processing rice for the market, and in time a "rice revolution" struck the low country with effects just as profound as tobacco's had been on the Chesapeake.

Western Africans played a role in South Carolina's move to a rice economy. Fair numbers of men and women from societies having long experience cultivating rice came to South Carolina before 1700. Such coastal groups as the Jola, Papel, Baga, Temne, and Mende from the Gambia River south past Cape Palmas produced wet rice for centuries prior to their contact with Europeans. So did inland peoples, the Bambara and Mandinka of the upper Niger in particular. Their methods of production were similar. They built dikes to catch water and turned soil with long-handled, flat-tongued instruments; planted with a hoe; sang in unison as they cultivated; winnowed with broad, flat baskets; and husked with mortar and pestle. These techniques came to be the ones used initially and disseminated among South Carolina plantations through the middle of the eighteenth century. Experienced slaves who were encouraged to produce their own provisions grew rice successfully while their masters were failing to do so. Planters eager to discover a staple to market would have been easy to convince of the efficacy of African techniques of rice production. Thus, knowledge of rice cultivation spread among South Carolina planters over a generation beginning in the 1690s.

For a brief time after 1700, South Carolina had one of the most diversified lists of exports in colonial America. Then rice overtook all the others. South Carolina exported 1.5 million pounds of rice in 1710, 6 million in 1720, and 20 million in 1730. By the 1720s it became the major low-country export, surpassing pitch and tar. South Carolina planters rushed to grow indigo during periods when war disrupted England's supply of better quality dyes from the French West Indies, but indigo production never rivaled rice over the long term. When around the middle of the century Carolina planters introduced a "tidal flow" method of rice production that regulated water on fields and prevented poor yields from drought, rice had become the low-country king. "The only Commodity of Consequence produced in South Carolina is Rice," noted the colony's governor, James Glen, in 1761, "and they reckon it as much their staple Commodity, as sugar is to Barbados and Jamaica, or Tobacco to Virginia and Maryland." By Glen's time the popular grain was accounting for 60 percent of all exports of the region.

Geography limited rice culture and affected the direction of its spread. Rice grew readily only in the lowest coastlands where tidal rivers irrigated the fields. This restricted its cultivation to a strip along the Atlantic seldom more than twenty miles wide. Southward along the Carolina coast rice culture spread rapidly, but that spread halted at the Savannah River, below which ownership claims with Spain were not clear.

It was along those more southerly coastal lands in 1732 that England chartered Georgia, a colony that was to reform England's dispossessed and criminal elements and be the basis for a society that saw virtue in hard work, temperance, and Christian morals. The Georgia Trustees banned slavery from the colony by legislation in 1734 because they believed slavery would hinder development of the virtuous, egalitarian society of small landholders they expected to create. So Georgia was free of slaves, more or less, through the first two decades of its existence.

Slavery might have come to Georgia eventually no matter what, but it was hurried along because of the failure of the inadequately prepared and poorly skilled white colonists to succeed at producing anything (wine, silk, and more) the trustees wanted. South Carolinians in particular began pressing Georgia's trustees and the English Parliament to make slavery legal in the colony. The trustees experimented with a more humane system of forced servitude in the 1740s, but by mid-century it fell before economic expedience. Thereafter, Parliament rendered Georgia free of restriction on slaveholding. Land-hungry South Carolinians were the first migrants into Georgia's coastal regions after 1750. They brought with them their know-how for producing rice and their labor force. Other groups followed and moved southward toward the St. Mary's River following Spanish cession of disputed land after 1763.

Low-country Georgians got most of their slaves via the South Carolina market until the middle 1760s. After that they began importing slaves directly from Africa. Like other colonies, Georgia had to wait until its market could dispose of whole cargoes before fully laden slavers would stop at its ports. By 1773 Georgia had a black population of around fifteen thousand, roughly equal the size of its white population. As in South Carolina, in Georgia's rice-producing region blacks outnumbered whites considerably. Because of the confinement of rice culture to the narrow coastal strip and of the difficulties Georgians had finding staple products to grow in the back-country, slavery in colonial Georgia remained exclusively a low-country institution. Georgia's 126-mile-long Rice Coast was also its Slave Coast.

The transformation to rice production in South Carolina and its spread to coastal Georgia brought about plantation agriculture on a scale not before known on the North American mainland, and the large plantation operations affected the working lives of the slaves. More than any other mainland area, the low country began to resemble the sugarcane islands in the British West Indies. Small farms were not as efficient as large, specialized plantations, so the latter became the norm.

The Atlantic trade had to bring in enormous numbers of Africans to maintain the size of the work force, but it responded to the demand. Between 1706 and 1776, ninety-four thousand slaves entered Charleston harbor for sale and disbursement throughout the low country. By 1740, in the oldest plantation areas north and south of Charleston, black slaves made up 90 percent of the population. The largest plantation owners grew exceedingly wealthy and spent time away from production, in Charleston or Savannah during winter months and perhaps in New England through the heat of the summer. Hired managers and overseers saw to the management of the plantation.

The difficult working and living conditions brought on by the switch to intensive staple agriculture led to rising rates of slave mortality in the low country. South Carolina physician Alexander Garden notified the Royal Society of Arts in 1755 of the situation:

... Tilling, Planting, Hoeing, Reaping, Threshing, Pounding have all been done merely by the poor Slaves here. Labour and the Loss of many of their Lives testified the Fatigue they Underwent, in Satiating the Inexpressible Avarice of their Masters, [who] ... pay ... dear for their Barbarity, by the loss of many ... Valuable Negroes, and how can it well be otherwise, the poor Wretches are Obliged to Labour hard to Compleat their Task, and often overheat themselves, then Exposing themselves to the bad Air, or Drinking Cold Water, are immediately ... Seized with Dangerous Pleurisies and peripneumonies ... which soon ... End their wretched Being here.

Masters were not particularly mindful of the results. Prices for imported Africans dropped a bit with increased supply, so masters could purchase healthy Africans to replace the deceased. When prices for rice fell, as they did with the rising production, planters' instincts were to clear more land, grow more rice, increase crop yield, and get more labor from the existing force—all of which meant worsening living conditions and greater morbidity for the slaves. Not until the eve of the American Revolution did the low-country slave population begin to sustain itself, and "salt water" slaves continued to flow into the colonies in large numbers.

As in other colonies, when the proportion of slaves to free persons began to rise, or even portended to do so, white anxiety mounted. The result in South Carolina and Georgia was the steady erosion of rights for blacks until they faced the strictest laws with the most harsh punishments of anywhere in the English mainland colonies. The process took place first in South Carolina, where in the 1690s the Assembly began borrowing from the slave codes of its "parent" colony, Barbados. White fears rose particularly, though, after the mid-1720s, when slave imports into the colony topped one thousand per year. As the Lords Commissioners for Trade and Plantations put it, "ye whole Province was lately in danger of being massacred by their Owne Slaves, who are too numerous in proportion to ye White Men there." "Suspicious gatherings" of blacks in the streets of Charleston set whites on edge, prompting the organization, in 1721, of a "Negro Watch" to stop slaves on sight (with instructions to shoot any black not stopping on order) and to confine blacks found on the street after 9:00 P.M. In the same year the colonial militia took over previously irregular patrols in rural areas. Powers of patrolmen were arbitrary and almost without limits. They could administer twenty lashes to a slave found off the plantation without authorization, search slave dwellings indiscriminately, and kill suspected runaways who resisted or fled. A system of justices of the peace for minor offenses and panels of justices and freemen for felonies maintained the appearance of formality in the seemingly contradictory realm of "slave justice." Punishments for those judged guilty were swift, severe, and frequently inhumane. They included castration; nose-splitting; chopping off of ears, hands, or toes; branding; or burning at the stake. Overseers and masters administered their own justice and punishment on the plantation, and those acts varied from reasonable to arbitrary and depraved.

Beyond the law, however, was social practice which limited slaves' lives and took away from the quality of their existence. Tension between the minority of white workers and the black majority manifested itself in the setting apart of specific jobs for each group. Whites limited blacks in the practice of skilled trades and set aside certain jobs as fit only for persons of color. Consequently, blacks, often the young, collected and disposed of all refuse, built most roads and cut canals, served as carters and stevedores, and even had duty as roughnecks to collect debts or settle masters' scores. Tensions mounted between white and black men over sexual relations. White preoccupation with the very notion of black rape grew through the century. The *South Carolina Gazette* tended to overlook white men ravishing black women, as happened with some regularity, but it devoted front page space to instances of black rape alleged to have occurred in distant colonies.

Yet there were hidden social and cultural advantages for blacks living on the isolated low-country rice plantations. Rice production required individual, demanding work on separate, quarter-acre plots; it lent itself to a task system of labor. Overseers gave individual slaves specific tasks to complete for a day's work. When finished the person had free time. This free time, which men and women worked hard to gain, enabled rice-plantation slaves to do things on their own, among fellow slaves, and usually away from the eyes of white society. They raised their own crops and poultry, made crafts, hunted and fished, sold their surplus wares or produce, and spent time being social with their peers. The effects of this isolation and limited free time were important in the development of a distinct culture among the low-country slaves—a culture that manifested much more of their African heritage than that of other blacks who were less isolated and had less personal freedom.

## New England and the Middle Colonies

After considering black slavery in the Chesapeake and low country, one tends to think of the much smaller number of blacks in New England and the Middle Colonies as relatively insignificant. After all, in 1770 there were barely fifty thousand individuals of African descent north of Maryland (not quite

4.5 percent of the total population) whereas in the same year from Maryland southward some four hundred thousand blacks made up 40 percent of the total. Blacks were only 2.5 percent of the New England population and 6.5 percent of the people in the Middle Colonies on the eve of the American Revolution. But figures alone fail to give an accurate picture of the importance of slavery to the economy of the area north of the Chesapeake and especially to particular regions of the area. In some of the most agriculturally productive rural areas of Connecticut, Long Island, and the lower Hudson River valley, blacks made up as much as half the work force. Certain industries—ironworking in Pennsylvania or tanning in New York, for instance—relied heavily on slave labor, and slaves worked in the carrying trade and around shipyards in Rhode Island and Massachusetts. In New England, blacks were concentrated near coastal urban centers along river systems. There was a particularly heavy concentration in Rhode Island. The Middle Colonies had black urban populations of considerable size. Thus, in certain areas the black population was a significant proportion of the total. In these areas blacks did not live in isolation from others of African descent and the demands and customs of whites did not totally dominate their lives.

In addition to sheer numbers, slavery in New England and the Middle Colonies was different in other obvious ways from the institution found on the mainland from the Chesapeake southward. Plantations never formed from Pennsylvania northward. If the typical southern African American lived and worked with a fair-sized group of other slaves on a large tobacco or rice plantation, the typical northern slave lived alone or with one or two others slaves, perhaps in a dwelling with the family of the owner, and worked on a small farm, in a small industry, as a domestic, or at a trade in an urban area. The origin of most northern slaves was different, too. Before 1740 it was rare for captives to arrive in a northern port immediately after the voyage from Africa. Most came from the West Indies or the southern colonies. Only between 1740 and 1770 was there direct importation of Africans into northern markets, and then the numbers of imports never approached those of the plantation colonies.

Reasons for the considerable differences of slavery in the northern colonies have to do with the northern economy. New England and the Middle Colonies never devoted most of their resources to production of a major staple to export. There was simply not one in demand they could produce. Instead, over time, northerners became efficient at a variety of tasks that, when combined, brought them the export credits they needed to keep in check their balance of trade. These tasks included grain and livestock farming, whaling and fishing, and the carrying trade. None of these tasks involved the same economy of scale that southern planters exercised. Even those producing food for export did so efficiently on family farms. There were exceptions, of course, but most producers relied on their own and their families' labor, and they tended not to gain the extraordinary wealth that would enable them to buy more laborers and expand operations.

But why, then, did settlers of the northern colonies get involved with black slavery in the first place, even in the small numbers they did? Part of the reason has to do with their early and extensive participation in the carrying trade of the Atlantic world.

Dutch colonists rather than the English were the first to import slaves north of Maryland. The Dutch West India Company, which carried out settlement of New Netherland along the Hudson River, established posts in the mid-1620s for the fur trade. The company may have desired development of a stable, agriculture-producing colony along the lower Hudson, but it refused to invest enough to prompt colonizers from the Netherlands to go there. Instead, it brought in workers before farmers. Always eager to introduce chattel slavery to New World colonies so it could enhance its brisk carrying trade in slaves, the company began in 1626 to import blacks into its own mainland colony. Most came from Curaçao in the Dutch West Indies. In addition to building roads and forts and raising food for the Dutch garrison in New Amsterdam, the slaves cleared lands along the Hudson. By midcentury enough slaves had entered the colony and rendered enough land arable to alter the nature of New Netherland. Only then did Dutch colonists begin coming to settle permanently, using the cleared lands for growing grain and keeping livestock. Farming replaced fur-trading as the principal colonial activity. The new farmers preferred slaves to free laborers largely for reasons of cost. In the 1640s a "seasoned" slave from the West Indies cost about the same as the wages, provisions, and lodging for a free worker for a single year.

The takeover of New Netherland by the English in 1664 did not alter the slaves' status. The earliest English laws in New York recognized slavery as a legal institution at the same time they placed restrictions on white servitude. As a consequence, demand for slaves increased, the slave trade from the islands and other colonies flourished, and New York's black population grew. By 1700 the colony had two thousand slaves in a population of about nineteen thousand and by 1750 the number had grown to ten thousand out of seventy-five thousand total—more than any other mainland colony north of the Chesapeake. Many of these were in the vicinity of New York City, where 43 percent of whites in a rough 1703 census owned one or two slaves. Because of their use as domestics, there were as many black women as black men among the slave population.

New York was not the only Middle Colony to which the Dutch West India Company brought slaves. Its ships carried small numbers of blacks to settlements along the Delaware River after 1639 and to the west bank of the Hudson that became part of New Jersey in 1664. English proprietors of New Jersey eventually authorized slavery and encouraged importation with offers of up to sixty acres for each slave brought to the colony. By the end of the century, Perth Amboy became one of the main ports of entry for northern slaves.

If Pennsylvania did not have slaves at the arrival of its Quaker founders in 1681, it did soon after. William Penn preferred black slaves to white servants "for then," Penn reasoned, "a man has them while they live," and he used slaves on his own estate. Philadelphia carriers in the Caribbean trade soon were bringing black men and women with return cargoes. The presence of Quakers there and in Delaware did not preclude slave imports. Philadelphia Quakers bought 150 Africans in 1684 to work clearing trees and erecting houses. By 1700 one Philadelphia family in fifteen owned slaves.

New England had fewer African Americans than any other region of the mainland colonies. Black slaves had been in New England since before 1640, however, and in some places they were important elements of the economy and society. Most black men and women came there because of coastal New England's interdependence with the West Indies and its heavy participation in the Caribbean trade. Ships arriving in New England ports from the British West Indies often carried half a dozen slaves. Some were "refuse" slaves (the infirm or ailing, who could not be sold profitably in the island markets), exiled offenders of various sorts, or those purchased to work the voyage northward and then sold upon its termination. More New England slave imports were African by birth than this implies, however. A slaver sometimes used the Caribbean islands as way stations, selling some of its captives and then passing on to New England with a partial load of Caribbean produce and the remainder of its slaves. New England masters seemed to care less than Tidewater planters about receiving the "bad lot" of slaves from the Caribbean, just as they showed less concern for place of origin of Africans. They believed they could train blacks individually and instill proper Yankee traits in the most reluctant slave. Thus, although most ships carrying slaves to the region came from the West Indies, probably three of four slaves imported into New England once had a home in Africa.

Nowhere in the northern colonies was the uneven distribution of blacks more evident than in New England. Because of the ties of slave imports to colonial shipping, major ports held concentrations of African Americans. In 1754 three quarters of Massachusetts's black population of twenty-seven hundred lived in coastal towns in only three counties. At the same time, blacks made up good portions of the population of Rhode Island's Narragansett ports—20 percent of Newport, 30 percent of South Kingston, and 40 percent of Charlestown.

Slavery in northern towns and cities from Salem to Philadelphia was different from most other forms of slavery in the colonies. Gary B. Nash's "Slaves and Slaveowners in Colonial Philadelphia" in his *Race, Class, and Politics: Essays on American Colonial and Revolutionary Society* (1986) provides a picture of who owned slaves in a northern colonial city and what the slaves did. In 1767 most Philadelphia masters (521) owned only one or two slaves (905 total). For many owners the bondsmen were a symbol of status. Merchants and shopkeepers owned one-third of the slaves; professionals owned 10 percent; innkeepers or tavern owners about 5 percent; and widows and "gentlemen" another 5 percent. Nearly all slaves from this last group were household servants. Artisans and craftsmen or men involved in maritime ventures owned the other half of the city's slaves. Bakers, ropemakers, brewers, millers, shipwrights, blockmakers, sailmakers, goldsmiths, and ferrymen used slaves in their work. A surprising number of ship captains and mariners (10 percent of all owners) purchased slaves with the intention of having them work on board ship as sailors.

None of this should give the impression that northern slavery was primarily an urban experience. As elsewhere, the vast majority of northern blacks lived and worked in the countryside. Most were agricultural workers on small farms, with the heaviest concentrations in Connecticut and Rhode Island, on Long Island, and in northern New Jersey. These farms raised provisions and draft animals primarily for export to the West Indies. Even here, white laborers made up a majority of workers on the seasonal crops. Through most of the year, African Americans worked around the masters' houses and stables. As in the cities, owning a slave was a mark of wealth and status.

Because African Americans were in much smaller proportion to the total northern population, control of slaves in most locales was less of a problem than it was in the southern colonies. Absence of laws regulating slavery did not reflect this so much as did lax enforcement. Slave codes in New England were probably the least stringent of all. There, slaves walked a fine line between being persons with certain rights on the one hand, and being pieces of property on the other. The result was ambivalence in colonial statutes. Massachusetts taxed slaves as persons *and* as property; Connecticut and Rhode Island taxed them as they did livestock. New England slaves could own, transfer, and inherit property at the same time their masters could sell and bequeath them. Puritan masters were especially inconsistent in dealings with their bondsmen. To them the slave was part of the master's family, so Massachusetts Puritans saw to it that slaves had "all the liberties and Christian usages which the law of God, established in Israel concerning such persons, doth normally require." However, Puritans regarded persons of African descent in Biblical terms, too, which meant, in the words of Cotton Mather, they were "miserable children of Adam and Noah." Strict in their response to all sexual matters, Puritans held particular abhorrence of miscegenation. The Massachusetts law banishing—usually to the West Indies—blacks guilty of fornication with whites was the most severe of such laws in any continental colony.

The Middle Colonies, where larger numbers of African Americans tended to congregate in cities, had more difficulty controlling their slave populations. Curfews and laws forbidding serving of alcohol to blacks were common; punishments were severe. New York had the most difficulty of northern cities. It had slave conspiracy panics in 1712 and 1741. The latter led to the arrest of fifty-four blacks and execution of thirty-one.

In spite of the body of legislation that governed northern slaves, their lives were not so proscribed as those of slaves in southern colonies. It was difficult in a town or city, where slaves worked as deliverymen, runners of errands, or hired artisans, to restrain movement and assembly. So authorities grew tolerant of curfew violations and gatherings of African

Americans that did not appear to presage trouble. Still, lack of enforcement did not reduce the total effect of the northern slave codes. "They cast a shadow everywhere," writes Edgar J. McManus in *Black Bondage in the North* (1973), "reminding slaves they were a caste apart, living on sufferance in a system amply geared for their destruction."

Beyond jurisdiction of the slave codes was a body of African Americans in the North who were free. Numbers of free blacks in the northern colonies were small, not much different from the numbers of free blacks in the southern colonies. In material ways, their existence was not considerably better than slaves in their midst. In some ways the existence of slavery hindered free blacks. Slaves who rose to responsible positions under their masters' employ posed no threat to white society, but free blacks who achieved important positions by themselves did. So whites took care to see that northern free black persons remained in menial jobs. Free black shopkeepers had difficulty getting credit; free black artisans were not always welcome in shipyards or at building sites. For those who were destitute it was more difficult in freedom than in slavery. In Boston of 1742 there were 110 free blacks in the almshouse and 36 in the workhouse out of the city's total black population, slave and free, of only 1500. If other immigrants to the mainland received rewards for hard work, thrift, and steady movement toward assimilation, Africans in colonial America suffered for such behavior at the hands of a white population that saw African American advancement as a threat to the established order.

## Slavery And Racial Prejudice

Consideration of the origins of slavery in the English mainland colonies leads to questions about the relationship between slavery and racial prejudice. Was English racial prejudice against black Africans the main reason slavery began? Or did the enslavement of Africans come first for economic reasons, and did the condition of slavery then lead to racial prejudice against those enslaved?

Investigation to answer these questions has centered on the Chesapeake, where English mainland colonists made the first legal commitment to black slavery and first practiced slavery on a large scale. The major problem investigators encounter has to do with the lack of acceptable evidence showing clear trends for the period before 1660. Good historians have examined existing evidence and concluded that English landowners treated their black and white servants alike. Others equally good have used the same evidence to find that the early English settlers had strong feelings of racial prejudice against Africans, concluding that this racism was the basis for the eventual development of black slavery as a major economic and social institution in the colonies. One historian, Winthrop D. Jordan, offers a middle ground in *White Over Black: American Attitudes Toward the Negro, 1550–1812* (1968). Enslaving blacks was an "unthinking decision," according to Jordan. "Slavery and 'prejudice' may have been equally cause and effect, continuously reacting upon each other, dynamically joining hands to hustle the Negro down the road to complete degradation." But not everyone has since agreed with this part of Jordan's book, and the issue remains unresolved.

The intellectual and emotional atmosphere surrounding the early English settlers of the Chesapeake had a considerable effect on the colonists' attitudes and thus bears on questions about the relationship between racial prejudice and the origin of slavery in Virginia and Maryland. For matters concerning race, the first colonists carried strong emotions—less so about Africans than about Native Americans. Although armed before arrival with ambivalent feelings about the persons they found living in the New World, once settlers craved the Native Americans' land, a hostile-savage-without-civilization image gained acceptance. Colonists assuaged their guilt over taking these lands by thinking of Native Americans as brutish, uncultured, without religion, nearer to beasts. They witnessed Native Americans being violent in the futile defense of their lands, and this reinforced English conceptions. By the 1620s, following massacres of encroaching settlers, Virginians were describing Native Americans as

> by nature sloathfull and idle, vitious, melancholy, slovenly, of bad conditions, lyers, of small memory, of no constancy or trust . . . , never looking what dangers may happen afterwards, less capable then children of sixe or seven years old, and less apt and ingenious.

Such ideas of a people physically different from the English developed rapidly throughout the mainland colonies.

English ideas about black Africans affected settlers' thoughts and actions, too. Before confronting Africans in America, most English had negative preconceptions of blackness and black people. Black signified things dark, sinister, evil and foul, whereas white suggested purity and virtue. Most Africans the English encountered were not just darker than they, as were Mediterranean people, but many were among the darkest people in the world, odd-looking individuals with strange customs to the English. They were not only un-Christian but seemingly without religion to an English world that found its basis on earth and beyond in religion. And Africans were apparently savage folk who dressed in few clothes, ate strange foods without utensils, and lived among odd beasts. So no matter where African immigrants arrived on the mainland, they were going to be entering a narrowly defined world charged with strong feeling toward themselves and those native to the land.

But was it primarily this racial prejudice that led English settlers to adopt slavery as the permanent condition for African immigrants to the mainland? More and more students of the period believe not. They believe, instead (and as argued in earlier portions of this chapter), that the colonists' failure to find elsewhere in North America the long-term, stable labor force they needed, coupled with the availability of large numbers of Africans at inexpensive prices, brought the colonists to opt for black slavery. Racial prejudice would help the English justify enslaving Africans some time later when they needed to do so, just as it helped them rationalize taking land from Native Americans, but perceived economic necessity was more the reason for the turn to black slavery.

Once slavery became a permanent condition for Africans in America, its effect on strengthening the existing racial prejudice was considerable. One racial group could hardly keep another in bondage without developing negative feelings against those enslaved. When it proved necessary to punish slaves beyond the limits English law allowed—as when Robert Carter (the same "King" Carter from the first page of Chapter One) could get an order from the Lancaster County (Virginia) court, as he did in March 1707, to cut off the toes of "two incorrigible negroes of his named Bambarra Harry and Dinah . . . for the better reclaiming the said negroes and deterring others from ill practices"—justification came in labelling the persons of African descent different from the white English. "It was not necessary to extend the rights of Englishmen to Africans," writes Edmund Morgan, "because Africans were 'a brutish sort of people.' And because they were 'brutish' it was necessary 'or at least convenient' to kill or maim them in order to make them work."

Across all classes of white colonial society, negative feelings toward African Americans grew. The very existence of black slavery provided a sense of separateness and unity to whites of gentry, middling, or commoner classes. It gave whites a common identity and then intensified their attitudes toward one of the other major identifiable groups on the mainland. The result within a few generations was a white society manifesting early forms of racial prejudice that would soon intensify and last for centuries, and a black population caught in a labor system that could only keep them at the bottom of America's economy and society. Gary B. Nash summarizes African Americans' plight in *Red, White, and Black: The Peoples of Early America*, second edition (1982):

Irrevocably caught in the web of perpetual servitude, the slave was allowed no further opportunity to prove the white stereotype wrong. Socially and legally defined as less than a person, kept in a degraded and debased position, virtually without power in their relationships with white society, Afro-Americans became a truly servile, ignoble, degraded people in the eyes of the Europeans. This was used as further reason to keep them in slavery, for it was argued that they were worth nothing better and were incapable of occupying any higher role. In this long evolution of racial attitudes in America, nothing was of greater importance than the enslavement of Africans.

# CHAPTER THREE

# African American Culture

Frederick Douglass, the gifted African American who escaped from slavery in 1838 and became one of the country's leading abolitionists, was born in Talbot County, Maryland, in 1818. Many know of Douglass and the difficulties he faced as a slave from *Narrative of the Life of Frederick Douglass, an American Slave*, which he wrote in 1845 to further the abolitionist cause. Much of the book is about his relationship with white masters and mistresses. There is little in the narrative about his family or the black community in which he lived.

In the late 1970s Dickson J. Preston began investigating Douglass's early life to determine how much of the *Narrative* he could verify with independent evidence. In *Young Frederick Douglass: The Maryland Years* (1980), Preston shows that Douglass

had not sprung full-grown out of nowhere, as his contemporaries seemed to think; his black ancestors, for a century or more before his birth, had been a strong and closely knit kin group with family pride and traditions that were handed on to him by his part-Indian grandmother, Betsey Bailey. His roots were anchored deeply in the earliest American experience.

Douglass's family was part of a black subculture of Maryland's Eastern Shore, itself a variant of a greater Chesapeake African American culture. Both were set into the broader unity of black culture in America. Both were tied closely to the Euro-American culture of whites, among whom African Americans lived, worked, worshipped, and played. Douglass was not unique among mainland North American blacks in his family origins or cultural surroundings. Throughout the mainland for several generations before Douglass was born, blacks were living in families and participating in different but related subcultures that were stable products of a long evolution in the colonies. The black American subcultures that appeared long before Douglass's birth were the result of interactions among Africans, Native Americans, and Europeans. What emerged were patterns of behavior and social customs that were distinctly African American.

## African American Community and Culture

Africans went through considerable change in the process of becoming African Americans. Slaves just arriving in America after the grueling voyage across the Atlantic were stepping into completely new physical, social, and cultural settings. Tired, sore, probably sick and poorly nourished, separated quickly from other Africans they had come to know on the voyage, they must have been bewildered and frightened of what was to come. Over a short time they had been forcibly detached from the kinship networks that had been their social, economic, and psychological underpinnings in western Africa. Never would they be more alone. Yet by 1770, African Americans throughout the mainland colonies were living in families with extended ties of kinship in greater black communities, and they were practicing a culture of their own. The development of African American families, communities, and a common culture took place during the first two-thirds of the eighteenth century in the English mainland colonies. These activities set the basis for black life in America from that time forward.

Slaves' early experiences were among the most difficult. For personal survival the new arrival quickly had to experience a degree of individual acculturation. Learning enough English to get by was the first task. On large plantations masters put new arrivals to work with slaves who already knew basic English and were aware of fundamental principles of the slave's existence. On smaller farms or other settings the newcomers learned from their masters or white servants. Through the first weeks they endured and changed. To a certain level the change was rapid.

To help cope with their new lives under difficult conditions, the uprooted Africans had their own cultural traditions and ways of doing things. These included a sense of personal identity; a language; a view of the world, which usually involved a religion; ideas of time and space, family life, and work; social customs; historical traditions; and a general know-how. Because slaves came from such a broad range of western Africa, they brought a variety of languages, customs, and traditions. They were not able simply to join together and practice group survival on the basis of their common heritage. However, they held in common enough ideas that they could mingle aspects of their cultures. For many this seems to have begun soon after capture in Africa or on shipboard. Once they arrived in the English colonies they continued this amalgamation as they began applying "old ways" to new circumstances. This process of clinging to and adapting certain of their traditional customs while borrowing heavily from Anglo-American and Native American ways would result, over time, in the development of a hybrid African American culture.

Not all newly arrived Africans went through a process of culture formation in the same fashion or at the same time and pace. For individuals the rate of acculturation varied according to a combination of factors including their local circumstances, the strength of their particular African cultural tradition, and the person's will. For groups the process varied more widely because individual survival did not require formation of a group culture. However, a single principle dominates consideration of the development of African American culture in colonial America. It is that blacks in America first had to have extensive social contacts with a substantial number of other blacks—they had to exist in black communities—before there could be a real development of group values, ways, and beliefs. Making it possible to pass these manifestations of culture along to subsequent generations was the black family, where adults could pass down to their children ways of doing things and values considered important for survival and good living.

For more than a century of black existence in the English mainland colonies, the obstacles in the way of African American community development and family formation were myriad. Simple demographic configurations—the number of blacks and the relative numbers of blacks and whites in specific locations—affected African American social relations. These numbers were determined largely by the nature of the economy and of the slave trade in a region at a given time. Without sufficient numbers of African Americans within a distance that would allow regular contact, blacks could not have a social life among themselves. There had to be a black population of some density and with at least enough freedom to interact by themselves.

Proximity to white colonists also affected African American social and cultural development. Contrary to the traditional image of American slavery, in many places in colonial America blacks lived, worked, and interacted daily and fully with whites. This was true not only for New England, but as far south as urban Charleston or rural Virginia. In the latter colony, even the wealthiest masters spent hours each day with their slaves, directing, working, punishing, cajoling, teasing, arguing, relaxing, laughing, and worshipping. African slaves in such close relationships with whites learned English, accepted Christianity, and practiced Euro-American customs—all with an African cast—more quickly than those who did not. Those living and working with larger numbers of blacks and fewer whites in more isolated conditions had more extensive social relations among themselves and greater adherence to their African customs. For them, acculturation toward an Anglo-American "norm" was slower and less complete.

Demographic configurations between American slaves born in Africa (and hereafter referred to simply as Africans) and those of African descent born in the New World and partly acculturated (the true African Americans or creoles) were important for community development and cultural change. Where slave imports from Africa were heavy over several years and a good proportion of a black population was made up of slaves born in Africa, the Africans remained separate and kept more of their traditional ways. Where the trade was light or involved a majority of "seasoned" slaves from the Caribbean, there was more unity among the partly acculturated black population and less survival of unaltered African customs.

Demographics and the slave trade also played a role in the ability of black populations to grow by natural increase and to maintain stable families. So long as the slave trade was bringing large numbers of slaves every year to a region of the mainland, black men continued to outnumber black women in that area. Knowing they could more cheaply purchase and train a male adult laborer from Africa than to rear one, owners in these regions did little to encourage marriage, procreation, and family life. They worked women as hard as men and allowed no time off for childbearing or rearing. Also, slaves suffered in the new disease environment and owners cared little for the health of their slaves. Replacements came cheaply. So when the slave trade was heavy, mortality rates were high and birth rates were low. Under such circumstances a slave society could not replace its numbers naturally, and the disproportionately high number of black men would continue. With more black men than black women and with interracial marriage illegal, it was impossible for most slaves to achieve a normal family life. (As in other ways, African American Anthony Johnson of seventeenth-century Virginia, noted in the previous chapter, was the exception. "Mary a Negro Woman," whom Johnson married, was the only woman living at Bennett's Plantation in 1625.) Through the first half century of settlement, because of unequal sex ratios and high death rates, few males, black or white, were able to marry. When the slave trade from Africa declined, slave populations began increasing their numbers through natural means and sex ratios became more balanced. Only then were families as the basis of slave communities on the cards.

Different circumstances for living and working affected community development, too. Slaves living on isolated plantations that were self-contained production units had less contact with Anglo-American culture than such persons on small farms growing provisions for local markets. Plantation slaves working under the task system had more control of their lives than those working in gangs under more watchful eyes, and their autonomy enabled them to hold onto more of their African culture. Over time, in certain regions, plantation life grew settled and slaves enjoyed mobility among plantations. African American communities centered on the plantation then could broaden and include others in the neighborhood.

Urban slaves may have had the greatest autonomy, but they also lived more closely with whites. Some were permitted to attain skills, live on their own, and hire their own time. In the urban atmosphere, where work requirements led to laxness in enforcing controls, black people mingled with white people at work and play. For them acculturation was rapid.

Thus, as different levels of slave importing (from the West Indies and from Africa) and different systems of slavery developed at various times in the separate regions of the English mainland, so did variant forms of African American culture. Throughout the colonial period distinct patterns of African American culture evolved in the three regions of the English mainland settlement: the Chesapeake, the Carolina and Georgia low country, and the northern colonies. Among the separate

African American cultures of each region, one could make subtle distinctions in different localities and at various times.

For the first seventy-five years of settlement in Virginia and Maryland, planters made distinctions more on the basis of class than race. Chesapeake blacks, mostly West Indian creoles, suffered the same hardships as white servants. Some of each group who lived long enough attained freedom and ownership of land. Blacks interacted with whites of their class in work, play, and sex. But a more open racial society did not last. The importation of large numbers of Africans after 1680 altered this rapid acculturation. By 1710 three-quarters of Chesapeake blacks were Africans, mostly men. The sexual imbalance made opportunities for family life difficult and cut birth rates. Furthermore, Virginia planters often sent new arrivals to the Piedmont frontier, where they lived isolated from the Tidewater and most creoles. The smaller number of creoles remained closer to their masters, working as domestic servants and skilled artisans, freer to travel and more comfortable in an Anglo-American culture. Thus, through the 1740s Virginia and Maryland had distinct African and creole slave societies.

But whatever potential there was in the Chesapeake for a long-term African-creole split did not last. Allan Kulikoff explains why in *Tobacco and Slaves: The Development of Southern Culture in the Chesapeake, 1680–1800* (1986). In response to the growing number of blacks, planters in the region forged a unity with lower-class whites. They lumped all blacks together and stifled creole opportunities. Then beginning in the 1740s the slave trade from Africa declined and a long period of black natural increase ensued. The African American population grew with a more balanced sex ratio and creoles soon predominated. At the same time, planters brought more slaves together on larger plantations and in places turned to wheat production, giving some African American men and women seasonal variety in their work and opportunities to learn skills and make broader contacts. This, and the development of a network of roads and markets, made possible slave interaction from different plantations. Eventually, families with links going back through generations and broader slave communities became possible.

Thus, in some parts of the Chesapeake by the time of the American Revolution, there existed a unified African American community with its own ways of life and the time and space to practice them. Individuals still did not have latitude in their personal actions. Blacks lived near their masters and under the watchful eyes of the white majority. In language, formal religion, and family structure they were more like Anglo-Americans than were most slaves to their south. There still remained the obvious problems for family stability. However, by this time many African Americans had close, broad kinship relations; had brought many African ways to their religious practice; and had their own forms of music and dance, diet and dress, and work and play that made their culture identifiable and distinct.

If the African American population of the Chesapeake drew together and became increasingly acculturated through the middle of the eighteenth century, its counterpart in the Carolina and Georgia low country grew into separate parts. For the first thirty years of coastal settlement, the mostly seasoned, imported slaves worked closely with their white owners and a seemingly mutual cultural exchange transpired. This cultural exchange in early South Carolina may have been more reciprocal and symbiotic than anywhere else in the English colonies. But the massive African imports that gave the low country its black majority after 1720 changed the direction of the evolution of African American culture. In Charleston a creole, largely mulatto slave community emerged. These creoles lived close to whites and were more privileged and more thoroughly acculturated than their rural counterparts. Yet in rural areas there was a growing black community that the slave trade was continually renewing—not with seasoned slaves but with Africans. Individual segments of this group centered on the rice plantations. Its members were independent and self-reliant. Working on the task system gave the slaves more time to be with fellow blacks, away from white authority. Their isolation and independence enabled them to hold onto more African speech patterns (and thus developed a mixture of English and certain western African languages that made up the distinctive form of English known as Gullah), religious practices, and social customs than any other African Americans on the English mainland. By 1770 the two groups of lowland blacks, urban creoles and plantation slaves, lived a more separate and different existence than many whites and blacks in the Chesapeake.

North of Maryland, a century of importing small numbers of seasoned slaves brought about by 1740 a stable society of African Americans largely attuned to Yankee ways. Unlike early black arrivals in other areas, northern slaves increased their numbers naturally, lived in families, often slept and ate in the house of the master, and more than anywhere else existed in a world dominated by white society. Those who worked on farms did not work in gangs with other Africans and had considerable freedom of movement. Also, a far larger proportion of black men and women in the northern colonies lived and worked in urban areas—with all the freedom afforded by that situation.

However, between 1730 and 1770, increased importing of Africans reoriented northern blacks' tendencies away from complete Anglo assimilation. Standing apart from northern creoles, the "raw" imports reacquainted their fellow African Americans with aspects of their long-forgotten African heritage. As a result, northern blacks consciously included African elements in their communities and incorporated African social customs and practices—especially in ceremonies, folklore, singing, dancing, and leisure activities. The greater autonomy of northern blacks enabled them to maintain African customs even as they conformed more than any others to the white culture that surrounded them. Their smaller numbers made it possible to do so without threatening their owners and white society.

Within each of the broad regions of colonial America's African American society there was variety in individual communities and in local customs and practices. Family practices, religious thought and modes of worship, resistance to bondage, work routines, and the folklife of people living together differed depending on a host of local circumstances. Examination of these manifestations of African American culture provides a sense of the variety within a culture group so easily lumped together and considered as static and virtually homogenous.

## Family

African American culture hardly existed in identifiable form anywhere in colonial America until after black families came into existence. The family was the place where community could begin. It was also the unit for educating and socializing the young. If adults were to create and adhere to common values and customs, it was in the family where they could transfer these to subsequent generations.

The family was especially important for African Americans, partly because of their African heritage. In western Africa kinship was the basis for all social organization. The extended family on the village level and broader kinship links across wider areas gave Africans their individual and collective identities. These institutions united people separated by space and provided material and psychological support that was essential for daily living. Loss of the kinship network was probably the most disruptive force in the African's enslavement and movement from the homelands. It follows that for Africans, recreating the family in America was especially important for gaining an individual identity and for achieving collective survival under the difficult circumstances of slavery.

Yet African American families were destined to be different from the families that had been part of the slaves' African heritage. Western African families tended to follow single lines of descent, through males or females but not both. This enabled brothers, sisters, aunts, uncles, and more distant relatives—all who shared a common ancestor—to identify with an enormous group of kin. Marriage united two such kin networks in relationships of obligation and responsibility, so Africans arranged marriages carefully and bound them together with family pressures and payments of bridewealth. Thus across western Africa, even crossing ethnic lines, was a grid of related kin groups that held society together much more tightly than political authority or ethnic loyalty and provided security for those involved. Even if slaves in colonial America could have practiced African-style unilineal kinship, it would have taken generations, and complete freedom in marriage and residence to recreate the thread that held together western African society. In the end it was impossible.

Not that Africans did not try. Even on slave ships they began seeking relatives. Children called friendly adults "uncle" or "aunt," and adults tended to look after younger children who were not blood relatives. Where slaves existed in some numbers on the English mainland there developed a broad pattern of slave children addressing all older slaves with kinship titles and regarding them as the equivalent of relatives. Younger slaves respected elders in the African fashion. Children who developed bonds to fictive kin had a broader community of support and were better able to cope following the death or sale of parents or other blood kin.

Eventually, however, not fictive kin but real family relationships provided the foundation for the African American community. Although regional differences in the process were considerable, it was during the eighteenth century that the black family came into existence and matured in English mainland North America. Once demographic circumstances—sufficient numbers of blacks in roughly equal proportions of men and women—made black families possible, what emerged was an English style nuclear family with monogamous marital relationships that traced descent through both parents. For the nuclear family to prevail, black Americans had to overcome considerable obstacles, the greatest of which was the regular movement of slaves and thus the separation of married adults from one another and parents from children. Kulikoff describes a continuing process of slave household and family development and redevelopment in eighteenth-century Virginia and Maryland, variants of which were probably typical of other areas:

A young [white] man tended to receive slaves from his parents or purchase them on the open market, thereby separating [slave] family members. If economic disaster did not intervene, his slaveholdings grew through natural increase, slave families were reestablished, and extended family networks developed. When the master died, the family's slaves were divided among heirs, and the process began again. Only during the second stage were slave families even relatively secure. At the same time, as generation followed generation, households, or adjacent huts, became increasingly complex and sometimes included grandparents, uncles, aunts, or cousins as well as the immediate family. Since other kin lived on nearby plantations, geographically dispersed kinship networks that connected numbers of quarters emerged during the pre-Revolutionary era.

But because of the obstacles in the way of smooth family development for blacks, and because of remnants of African family patterns, black families in America only partially resembled the nuclear families of English colonists. It was common for African American families to live apart, for instance. Men often lived in separate households—out of necessity in areas of small black population—and women frequently played the most important roles in child rearing. Some blacks did not have attitudes toward sex and monogamy in accord with the wishes of their Christian masters. Premarital sex in limited practice was the norm in some western African societies, and so were freer sexual connections in polygynous marriages. Some African Americans seem to have clung to African sexual customs in their largely monogamous relationships, often to the consternation of their masters, white church officials, and others who believed promiscuity a flawed part of the black's natural makeup.

Few masters thought it necessary to bother with legality in slave marriages, but many of the African American men and women involved regarded the ceremonies as important and binding. Marriage rites varied and seemed to have meant as much as the couples desired. There were occasional Christian marriages for blacks, especially in New England, but common-law marriages, called "Negro marriages," were the norm. Farther south, slaves conducted their own ceremonies and such symbolic practices as "jumping the broomstick" united African American men and women.

Slaves knew family security was tenuous. The death of a master or a sharp economic downturn could mean sale and separation. Relationships between slave men and women were tempered with the knowledge that masters paid little heed to family status or personal appeals when they had sexual designs on a woman slave. Plaintive appeals mattered little also when a sale of slaves promised to break up a family. Masters frequently regarded the African American mother and her young children as a unit, separating them from their husband and father with little concern. Contemporary newspapers carried the evidence in advertisements of slaves for sale: "likely Negro wench, about 22 years old and a child about four years old. . ."; "likely Negro wench with a likely male child, ten months old"; "A Negro woman age about 24 years, and her child, a girl about five years." The *Boston News Letter* of May 1, 1732 listed for sale a nineteen-year-old African American woman and her infant son, to be sold "together or apart."

Yet it is probably inaccurate to describe slave marriages or slave families as "unstable" with the implication that contemporary white marriages and families were necessarily more "stable." Granted, not as many black husbands as white husbands lived with their wives and children, especially on small farms, and black families were always liable to forced separation, a master's sexual incursions, and more, but the older and more established colonial African American society became, the more black husbands lived with their families. However, simply because a man (black or white) resided with his wife and children, it did not necessarily follow that he cared greatly for any of his coresidents, nor did cohabitation automatically make for a "stable" or "secure" family. It is also not fair or safe to assume that a man living apart was one who cared little for his family or failed to nurture a loving group. White husbands of the time were not ones to involve themselves in child rearing. Many white men who resided "at home" spent hours or days away. William Byrd of Westover spent more waking time with those he called "his people," his black work force, than with his white family. Conversely, some black husbands who lived in quarters away from their families found ways to visit at nights and on Sundays and holidays, giving them, perhaps, as much intimate contact as some whites who resided with their families. In addition, some African American women seem to have had close ties with their children that were rewarding for both. One should not suppose that white women did not have such close ties, but tendencies of upper-class whites to hire nurses and nannies for their young children may have meant that some white women did not have the close and fulfilling relationships with their children that some black women had—forced separation notwithstanding.

The best evidence of the strength of ties among black family members in colonial America is in advertisements for slave runaways. One-third of the slaves mentioned in 589 Virginia advertisements before 1775 ran off to rejoin members of their families who lived in the vicinity, and the proportion of Maryland slaves who stole away for the same reason between 1745 and 1779 may have been higher still. "His parents are free and live in Port-Royal," read a Virginia advertisement; "he is about Mr. Samuel Thomae's in Warwick County, where he has a father and grandmother," read another; and a third read, "supposed to be harboured by Colonel John Snelson's Negroes . . . among whom he has a wife, or by his Brother, John Kenny, a Mulatto Slave belonging to Mr. Thomas Johnson of Louisa." According to Gerald W. Mullin in *Flight and Rebellion: Slave Resistance in Eighteenth-Century Virginia* (1972), "owners' understatements [in advertisements] indicate a depth to slave family life—and the whites' tacit recognition of that life—that up till now has not been dealt with in inter-pretations of American Negro slavery."

## Religion

Religion was the heart of African American culture in colonial America. African slaves came to the New World with strong religious beliefs and thoughts of the afterlife. In the American colonies they encountered masters and Christian ministers, Puritans and Anglicans, Methodists and Baptists, who were intent (in varying degrees, at different times, and mostly where it was useful to white society) on making them Christians. But religious belief is personal, often developed individually, and the private world of religion was a place slaves could turn during the periods of anxiety and stress that were such a large part of their lives. Thus, religion for African Americans was a blending of African religious practice and Christian belief, and it was a source of individual strength and collective se-curity through the eighteenth century as African American cul-ture matured.

African religions were not at all alike, but many western Africans held broad patterns of belief in common. (In the cases of some manifestations of belief—spirits, magic, taboos, use of amulets, and more—they shared ideas with common English people of their day as well.) The living bodies of western Af-ricans held their spirits, which, upon death, returned to a greater spiritual world where they joined those of their ances-tors. They believed spirits were about in inanimate objects—trees, rocks, hills, rivers—and these forces controlled much of the workings of the world. Ancestors intervened in the world of the living. Acts of placation, magic, and taboos were im-portant in controlling spirits and ancestors. Workers of magic were manipulators of spirits, often through the manufacturing of amulets and charms, and thus were powerful people in the African world.

In the New World, blacks received Christian teaching in more or less strenuous doses at different times and in various locales. Owners often opposed attempts to make slaves Christians, masking fear of loss of control of their property with arguments of insufficient black intellect for the religion or inappropriateness of doctrine. Following the lead of New Englanders, however, many whites came to believe that slavery was part of God's plan for bringing "heathens" out of Africa and giving them "knowledge of the True God." In this spirit, Protestant missionaries filtered through colonial America after the first quarter of the eighteenth century and attempted to instruct slaves in the "proper faith." To many slave owners this was a selection of Christian teachings that stressed meekness, humility, obedience, discipline, and work. Brotherhood of man or the escape of the Hebrews from bondage was noticeably absent from the Gospel according to the master.

It is ironic but instructive that, generally speaking, the more closely blacks worshipped with whites, the less they wanted to become Christians. Those who did worship with whites and still converted, however, practiced a form of Christianity that paralleled closely their Anglo-American fellow Christians. The opposite was also true. Where there was greater distance between master and slave in religious practice, blacks were more eager to become Christian, but their Christianity was different. It was much more a blending of African and European religious practices and beliefs.

In New England, for example, where social interaction was greatest and Christian proselytizing strongest, the majority of African Americans remained outside the white church. Only 3 percent of Newport, Rhode Island, blacks were Christians in good standing in 1775, and only a quarter of them attended church at all. This was so because, in spite of proselytical intentions that seemed noble, New England whites segregated blacks in church and treated them as second-class Christians in worship. Requirements for black baptism were especially rigorous. They included having theological knowledge as well as a Christian demeanor. Sermons to African American congregations justified the proper relationship between master and servant. Most important, slave owners refused to allow their bondsmen to worship by themselves for fear of the "mongralization" of Christian practices they thought was bound to occur. The failure to make good Christians of more than a tiny minority of African Americans "was not so much that Yankee masters did not tell their servants about Christianity," observes William D. Piersen in *Black Yankees: The Development of an Afro-American Sub-culture in Eighteenth-Century New England* (1988), "but that the Christianity they offered was self-serving and neither emotionally nor intellectually satisfying to most Africans and Afro-Americans." Those who did not convert practiced their own folk religion that was the kind of blending they preferred.

Farther south, African Americans learned of Christianity from their fellow slaves most frequently, but also from their masters, missionaries, and regular clergy. Worship often was with lower-class whites. An important difference from the northern colonies, however, was that southern whites either allowed their slaves more freedom to worship alone in ways they chose, or, as in the Chesapeake, they accepted enough African religious practice themselves to form a blend of Christian worship satisfactory to both. In Maryland and Virginia especially, but also in the Carolinas and Georgia, the middle decades of the eighteenth century, the time of the so-called Great Awakening, when an evangelical movement swept out of England and quickly reached the lands of southern slaveholders, was a special time for slave conversions and a blending of African and English modes of worship. Poor blacks and whites joined in worship and song in small prayer houses throughout rural Virginia. Together they proclaimed and witnessed and had emotional religious experiences. Many southern slaves considered themselves good Baptists, Methodists, Presbyterians, or Anglicans. But in the end they practiced a religion like the African American folk variety in New England.

In the African American folk religion blacks blended African religious practice into their expression of Christian faith. They held onto an idea that upon death one's soul went to one's homeland, almost always in the ground rather than in the sky. Funerals prepared the deceased's spirit for entry into the world of the ancestors. They were loud, raucous, joyous affairs with music, singing, dancing, laughing, and drinking. African Americans' practice of worship could involve soft singing or frenzied behavior. Presbyterian minister Samuel Davies, who was important in bringing the Great Awakening to blacks in Hanover County, Virginia, at the middle of the eighteenth century, recorded how African Americans' religious singing affected him spiritually:

March 2, 1756. Sundry of them [the Negroes] have lodged all night in my kitchen; and, sometimes, when I have awakened about two or three a-clock in the morning, a torrent of sacred harmony poured into my chamber, and carried my mind away to Heaven. In this seraphic exercise, some of them spend almost the whole night.

But religious ecstasy was more characteristic of organized services. Leaders of African American congregations exhorted their listeners and sought emotional response. Singing and dancing, standing and shouting were important parts of the services. Blacks (and whites) frequently had spiritual experiences—visions of ancestors, journeys to other times and places, encounters with God or the devil, views of heaven or hell. A common experience was spiritual death and rebirth, bringing about heightened religious feeling. Efforts to control spirits were manifested in amulets and charms worn for protection. Black mediums who made the charms became powerful persons in the black community. Through frenzied worship and spiritual experiences, African Americans were able to choose from Christian worship the stories from the Old Testament that made them feel a chosen people and allowed them to love their fellow humans in situations where being loving was not a natural tendency.

## Resistance, Escape, and Rebellion

A spirit of resistance and the potential for escape or rebellion ran deep in the colonial slave population. Proof of this is in the body of laws that existed to prevent such action. As slave populations grew, suspicion, distrust, and fear filled the minds of white colonists and became manifest in colonial statutes. Eighteenth-century slave codes limited the number of blacks who could meet in groups, forbade their carrying anything resembling weapons, kept blacks on the farm or plantation and off streets after dark, and even outlawed drums or horns, "which may give notice to one another of their wicked designs." Capital offenses included arson, poisoning, repeated theft, inciting insurrection, and resisting interrogation. Police watched urban blacks, slave patrols guarded rural areas, and white colonists remained vigilant. Local justices could resort to the equivalent of medieval torture to keep the slave population docile, but it was masters and overseers who most frequently corrected slave misbehavior in ways the law allowed. Colonial statutes permitted branding, flogging, burning, amputation of limbs, hamstringing, and execution. Records of administration of these punishments are wondrously matter-of-fact. Middlesex County, Virginia, in the first twenty-five years of the eighteenth century was probably typical. During that period the government saw to the sale of eight blacks to the West Indies (with compensation for their owners) for "frequent disorderly meetings." A minister and two accomplices beat to death the clergyman's slave for running away. A vengeful slaveowner castrated one slave for "running away, lying out and distroying peoples Stocks"; cut off the toes of another for "lying out and doing Severall Misdemeanors"; and pilloried and cut off the ears of a third for a second offense of stealing. Another Middlesex court executed a slave for treason, dismembering him and hanging one of his quarters in a public place to deter others.

In the face of such punishments, slaves were imminently practical. Forms of resistance ranged along a continuum from feigning illness or malingering to organized, mass, armed rebellion. The particular form resisting slaves selected depended on its chances for success, but the extent of slaves' acculturation and the kind of work they did also had a strong bearing on the ways they resisted.

"Saltwater" slaves had a tendency on arrival to run away with others who spoke the same language. However, it did not take them long to grasp the reality of their situations. Slaves not long in the colonies, still without much command of English and living an isolated existence with few other slaves, resisted in subtle ways. They ruined crops, broke tools, malingered and balked, feigned sickness or stupidity, or stole goods or animals for sale on the black market. Household slaves under closer supervision simply worked slowly, acted surly, or got drunk regularly. Alcohol consumption among certain groups of slaves was considerable. Most blacks not fully acculturated who did run away were more truant than long absent. Their limited ability to exist unnoticed in white society made them "outliers" upon escape. They hid in the woods and stuck close to the people they knew.

The more assimilated slaves became, the more wise they were to the ways of English colonists and thus the more capable of successful escape. Skilled artisans who were fully acculturated and moved freely between rural and urban environments were the ones most likely to try to escape from slavery altogether. Carpenters, "fishing Negroes," and boatmen were especially apt to run away for good. There was no northern freedom to run to, of course, but these runaways often headed for towns where they could get lost among the handful of free blacks and lower-class whites that made up the substratum of society. The North Carolina piedmont, populated by non-slaveholding whites, was another haven for fugitives. So was Spanish Florida. They ran away alone, many to rejoin relatives, and they relied on their skills and savvy to get jobs and carry on new lives.

Outright rebellion occupied the extreme end of the resistance-rebellion spectrum. Herbert Aptheker in *American Negro Slave Revolts* (revised 1969) notes that periods of widespread slave rebelliousness came in waves every generation or so, "as though anger accumulated and vented itself and then a period of rest and recuperation was needed before the next upsurge." There seem to have been waves of general slave unrest between 1710 and 1722, 1730 and 1740, 1765 and 1780, and 1790 and 1802. If full-scale rebellions were not occurrences of every few years, when they did happen they gained notice in colonial society sometimes out of proportion to their significance. Here again, chance of success was a guiding principle. African Americans greatly outnumbered by whites thought better of joining insurrections. Because this was frequently the case in the English mainland colonies—different from most other New World slave societies, where slave rebellions were more common—incidents of open rebellion were relatively rare. Still, since colonial publications did not spread word of conspiracies and insurrections, there is a sense that more were planned than most white colonists (and, subsequently, most historians) perceived. New York City was the scene of slave conspiracies, as was Charleston. Benjamin Franklin seems to have captured the general tone of some urban slaves when he described Philadelphia blacks as being of a "plotting Disposition."

The slave uprising that began near the Stono River, within twenty miles of Charleston, South Carolina, on September 9, 1739 was the most serious of the colonial period. This was so in large part because it triggered other rebellions and acts of resistance over several years. Newly arrived slaves from Angola planned the Stono Rebellion. Under the leadership of a slave named Jemmy, twenty blacks broke into a store, where they stole small arms and powder, killing the storekeepers and leaving their severed heads on the front steps. By daybreak, as they moved southward along the road toward Georgia and what seems to have been their ultimate objective, Spanish Florida, they had killed eight whites. Through the early afternoon they killed most of the whites they encountered—they spared a white tavern keeper who was known for his kindness to his slaves—and burned houses. Around midday the group, whose ranks had swollen to fifty or sixty, met up with South Carolina's Lieutenant Governor, William Bull, returning to

Charleston for the commencement of a new legislative session. Bull apparently had to ride hard to escape with his life.

After halting in an open field in midafternoon, the rebels, according to a contemporary "Account of the Negroe Insurrection," "set to dancing, Singing and beating Drums to draw more Negroes to them." Although before evening a force of mounted planters attacked and dispersed the gathering that at one time may have approached one hundred persons, it took nearly a week for a white militia company to catch and overcome the largest remnant of the group. Individual rebels were not apprehended for several months after the uprising began, and one leader remained at large for three years. Altogether, thirty whites and forty-four blacks died in the slaughter associated with the insurrection. The spirit of rebellion remained in the air for several years afterward. This uprising prompted South Carolina to lump together all blacks as dangerous to white society, whether "of a rebellious nature" or not, and systematically tighten restrictions (on free blacks and slaves) with the harshest penalties of any mainland colony.

Through the middle of the eighteenth century, newcomers from Africa seem to have been the ones most likely to join in rebellion. Thereafter, open rebellion was something plotted by the most highly assimilated slaves in the colonies. Mullin in *Flight and Rebellion* explains the irony of slave rebellions being tied to the acculturation process. As slaves acculturated according to their masters' designs, they learned their roles on the farm or plantation or in the house or factory, but they also learned strategies that would help them rise against their owners. Late in the colonial period the liberal influence of the American Revolution and the increased need for skilled slaves around cities led to a relaxing of restraints upon African Americans in urban areas. Freer to meet and more able to plan, it was these slaves who in 1800 organized "Gabriel's Rebellion," which Mullin considers "the most sophisticated and ambitious slave conspiracy" in American history. Acculturation, he concludes, "ultimately created slaves who were able to challenge the security of the society itself."

## Daily Life

If one thing dominated the daily lives of African Americans in colonial America, it was work. English traders brought men and women from Africa and colonial landowners and businessmen purchased these people to be the colonial labor force, so work they must. It was the rare master who did not want to get as much labor from his slave as he possibly could. But Africans received none of the rewards of their labors, so they lacked incentive to work. What had to result was a form of accommodation between master and slave.

Complicating accommodation was that the English master and the African in bondage brought different ideas about the pace of work and the amount of toil one should expect from a human. By the seventeenth century, English landowners and shopkeepers were becoming increasingly aware of the need to use time efficiently and to make strict accounting of time spent at work. They expected their servants to work from dawn to dusk with breaks only for meals. Before coming to America, upper-class English had difficulty getting what they considered a decent amount of labor out of their "lazy" workers, whose more popular, traditional, quasi-medieval notions of the length of a day's work and its pace differed considerably—and probably naturally—from those of their employers. West Africans' ideas of work were like English servants'. Their ways were practical for the heat of the tropics, based on patience, slow movement, waiting, time to relax and be social. Where possible work was communal and involved singing and talking. It also involved resting. In many West African societies, women did heavier agricultural labor and worked more steadily than men throughout the year. Men did some such work, and they protected their villages and served in positions that required them to manage family and village affairs, but a general and widely accepted goal for African men—especially of the higher classes—was not having to do great amounts of physical toil. It is not surprising then that English planters agreed generally with Virginia slave owner Landon Carter's assessment of it being "almost impossible to make a negro do his work well. No orders can engage it, no encouragement persuade it, nor no Punishment oblige it."

White slave owners went to great lengths to exact more work from their bondsmen. Instructions to overseers were explicit on how to do so. It required vigilance and punishment. But master and overseer could push too hard, and when they did slaves had valuable chips for the bargaining. Too much coercion often resulted in sick workers, broken tools, sloppy (and thus costly) work. Sometimes the consequences were more serious. A group of South Carolina slaves, retaliating for being worked far into the night, set fire to their master's barn and burned it and its contents to the ground.

Compromises over work took into account the seasonal nature of agriculture. A day's work was longer when tobacco needed topping or hoeing, or when rice needed harvesting. Once tobacco was hung in the tobacco house, rice barreled, or corn in, work rhythms changed. If most owners accepted the sunup-to-sundown principle, the rigor of its application varied with the crop cycle.

Slaves seem to have worked more steadily on small farms, where they toiled alongside the master. On large plantations where overseers were involved, slaves became particularly adept at manipulation. If allowed to work at their own pace they appeared satisfied, but they troubled overseers who drove them hard and complained to their masters of misuse. But no matter where they worked, a good bit of the Africans' sense of time and pace persisted. No less famous a planter than George Washington knew of the dangers to plantation efficiency and production of allowing blacks to set the pace and ways of work. He instructed a new manager to be wary of

an error which I have felt no small inconvenience from; and that is, that rather than persevere in doing things right themselves, and being at the trouble of making others do the like, they will fall into the slovenly mode of executing work which is practiced by those, among whom they are. I have experienced this not only from European tradesmen, but from farmers also, who have come from England and none in a greater degree than Mr. Whiting, and one Bloxham, who preceeded him; and who, tho' perfectly acquainted with every part of a farmer's business; and peculiarly so . . . in the management and use of Oxen for the Cart or plow, double or single, with yokes or with harness; yet, finding it a little troublesome to instruct the Negros and to compel them to practice of *his* modes, he slided into theirs. . . ."

It was rare when slaves did not get evenings and Sundays to themselves. They could practice their religion on Sundays, rest, tend to their garden plots, and go visiting. Holidays worked into the compromise, too. The biggest holiday that blacks and whites celebrated together was "Harvest Home." Western Africans and English always had their biggest feasts once crops were in, and the two had coinciding celebrations that involved eating, drinking, and general merriment.

Some masters realized that slaves worked best when they had authority and made decisions. Thus, there were plantations with hierarchies of black workers—directors of others and slave "drivers." Others, especially low-country masters, used the "tasking system" to set out acceptable work limits and to make sure that the slave who did a good amount of work got time for his or her own work or diversion.

A common misconception is that rural slave women, who could serve as house servants, had an easier time of it than their male counterparts. The opposite is closer to the truth. Many western African men and women came to the New World with ideas about women's place. It was in constant, fairly heavy labor, and African Americans seem to have joined masters in perpetuating the idea in the colonial world of work. In the plantation colonies nearly all black women worked in the fields, plowing, hoeing, and harvesting. By 1750 perhaps one slave woman in twenty from Maryland to South Carolina was strictly a house servant. The proportion was greater on larger plantations and practically nil on small farms. Moreover, women bore children under difficult circumstances. Midwives coated the umbilical stump with mud, sometimes causing tetanus, and stood the woman erect and shook her violently immediately after giving birth to deliver the placenta. It is not surprising that death of the mother in childbirth was common. Women cooked for their families (in an age, lest we forget, when "cooking" meals meant building fires and hauling water, and took considerable time and effort in preparation) and cared for the young. Old age was no respite. Elderly male slaves "retired" to the homestead when their field-working days were over, but old slave women simply got moved to domestic work, child caring, weaving, spinning, or dairying, so younger women could be free to work in the fields.

Similarities existed among the regions in the evolution of the black work force and in the tasks that slaves performed. With the exception of Africans who brought with them such usable skills as rice-growing, livestock-tending, weaving, or fishing and boating, unseasoned Africans knew the least about their labors. Masters had to give them simple tasks and to keep close watch on them. Creoles were more aware of how to perform jobs and they knew more about the constraints on resisting. Masters gave creoles more autonomy and sometimes more authority over their work, so that physically and emotionally their working lives were better than those of Africans.

Slaves practiced skilled trades at different times throughout the colonies. Those on small farms in New England or in urban areas always did a variety of tasks. Some of these individuals were the original jacks-of-all-trades. The more diversified economies of northern colonies or urban areas required a broader range of skills, and whites in these places often felt less threatened if African Americans performed skilled work. Lists of skilled roles slaves played are long and range from barber, blacksmith, and bookbinder to watchmaker, weaver, and whitesmith. In Charleston slaves dominated stalls in the public markets. Use of slaves as skilled craftsmen came more slowly to some areas of the plantation colonies. As late as 1733, nine of every ten slave men and probably all slave women in a Maryland county were field hands. But eventually, as larger proportions of southern slave populations became native born and as the growing plantations demanded craftsmen of all sorts, African Americans began practicing more skills. By the first third of the eighteenth century in some places, large plantations were becoming self-contained production units with slaves doing the necessary artisanal work as well as producing the crop. In 1768 James Grant of South Carolina could write, "In established Plantations, the Planter has Tradesmen of all kinds in his Gang of Slaves, and 'tis a Rule with them, never to pay Money for what can be made upon their Estates, not a Lock, a Hing, or a Nail if they can avoid it." Blacksmithing, butchering, carpentry, cooperage, and sewing were skills essential to most farms and plantations, and over time slaves on the larger units began weaving, cobbling, tanning, masoning, and distilling. By the time of the American Revolution, African Americans were performing these functions in all of the English colonies.

One particular group of skills, those that related to the water, were ones Atlantic West Africans brought to the mainland and used all along the coastal settlements from the earliest times. In New England they worked as sailors. Carolina plantations had "fishing Negroes," and throughout the southern lowlands African Americans manning skiffs and lighters were the heart of a transportation system that carried plantation goods to market, brought imported wares back from ports, and ferried whites across the maze of coastal waterways and landings.

The crux of slavery, however, was that no matter how good a slave got to be at work, no matter what skills the black person acquired, the fruits of the labor belonged to the master. If a slave reached a level of proficiency in a skill in great demand, or if field labor came to be in oversupply, as it did on some plantations after 1750, the master might "hire out" a slave to provide additional income. Hiring out was especially prevalent in northern colonies or in grain-producing areas where landowners had seasonal labor requirements and could not afford to keep large numbers of slaves year around. In some areas, masters hired out women slaves more frequently than men. After the 1750s in the Chesapeake, a small but growing number of slave artisans hired their own time—that is, they were allowed to live by and fend for themselves, finding their own work and paying their masters a weekly or monthly fee. Blacks normally received lower wages than whites for the same work, but it seems clear they liked hiring out their own time. They worked and mingled with a wider range of people and appreciated the relative freedom.

As the eighteenth century wore on, slaves played an increasingly important role in industry. In New England, African Americans worked in shipbuilding and such related industries as rope and sail making. They were involved in much of the building construction in towns or rural areas. Also, they mined coal and iron and worked many of the iron forges and furnaces in the colonies. In the 1770s slaves performed most of the skilled and manual labor in Chesapeake iron industries. Larger than most tobacco farms, these industries employed 1 percent of all adult slaves (women as well as men) in the Chesapeake. If the ironworks were representative, industrial slaves were the most privileged black laborers in the colonial period. They worked five-day weeks on average, were paid for work they did on the other two days, had access to goods in company stores, and had more freedom of movement than typical persons in bondage.

Technology played an important role in the working lives of slaves. Early technology in most places was simple and seemed to be of mixed English and African origin. Englishmen had ways of doing agricultural work they thought best, but so did Africans. It was difficult for masters and overseers to dictate the kinds of tools the work force used, and for a long time they did not. Africans devised many of the tools for rice production based on their African experience, and they clung, sometimes proudly and tenaciously, to their ways of threshing with hooped poles instead of "proper flails" until overseers stopped trying to change them. African workers had "perseverance" and "Greatness of Soul," overseers noted, referring to their adherence to their own farming methods. Slaves on some Chesapeake lands did not use carts and plows, as English farmers had done for centuries, until after 1750. Once carts and plows became commonplace, though, slaves were better able still to regulate the pace of work. The slaves could work slowly for periods and then catch up quickly with the new implements.

Although masters controlled slaves and held almost boundless legal authority to exact labor from them, no statutes nor pressures could bring humans to perform endless toil. What developed were patterns of labor that accommodated master and slave. If the latter had to work, the former could not alone define quantity and quality. It was a black world of work, Mechal Sobel reminds us in *The World They Made Together: Black and White Values in Eighteenth-Century Virginia* (1987), and African Americans had much to do with setting the standards in their world.

## Folk Culture

The idea that most slaves lived in "Negro quarters," clusters of dwellings set off by themselves resembling tiny villages, is out of time and place for the colonial period. Permanent groupings of slave quarters existed only on the largest plantations and were a development of the last quarter of the eighteenth century. In tobacco-growing Maryland of 1720, slaves lived scattered about the countryside in relatively isolated groups of half a dozen adults with their children. Even on large plantations prior to 1750, masters divided their lands into "quarters" and housed groups of slaves on each to allow them to be near the fields they tended and to spread livestock for grazing. Through the first half of the eighteenth century in Virginia, when male slaves outnumbered females, barracks-like structures housing six or more men were common. Small planters' field hands slept in barn lofts, tobacco houses, or other outbuildings.

Some slaves relied on African building styles as much as English forms in constructing their dwellings. Houses generally were square and small, perhaps twelve by twelve feet on average—and they were seldom permanent structures, allowing for movement with seasonal crops, fallowing, or removal from waste pits. They built the houses of wood mostly, though not entirely. In coastal Georgia they used a cement-like mixture of lime, crushed oyster shells, sand, and water called "tabby." Also, archaeologist Theresa A. Singleton (in "Breaking New Ground," *Southern Exposure*, 15, 1988) reveals "striking evidence" from excavations at eighteenth-century sites in South Carolina of African-style dwellings built with mud walls and thatched roofs. Slaves typically slept on straw bedding set on earthen floors and cooked by fires under wooden chimneys. They fetched water from springs, which were sufficient for most locations. Dwellings tended to grow in size and improve in construction, with such amenities as brick fireplaces, during Revolutionary times.

In northern colonies, more slaves lived with their masters, some in back rooms or attics of the same houses but more often in small outbuildings. As Boston, New York, and Philadelphia grew, late in the century, cheaply constructed tenements appeared and blacks moved in. At the end of the colonial period one could see the beginning of the movement of blacks into the southern part of Philadelphia, presaging a larger movement of subsequent decades that would plant the seeds for the city's nineteenth- and twentieth-century black neighborhoods.

Slaves' material standard of living was lean but not static. They were not to own property in most places, but when they stayed in the same place for some time they made furniture or acquired utensils. The longer they remained in one place, the more material goods they had to use. Slave clothing was fairly standard. Men wore shirts and trousers, women shifts tied at the waist, all made of coarse linen and homespun wool and cotton. Men wore hats while working in the field; women wore handkerchiefs. Both worked barefoot in the summer, but all had shoes for cooler times. No one considered undergarments a necessity, and socks were a luxury. Wealthy masters dressed personal servants better, in waistcoats and petticoat breeches. Artisans often earned enough to buy finer cloth and generally to dress better. Those who could afford to do so brought an African eye for color to their garments. Piersen notes in *Black Yankees* that the African Americans' style of dress in New England "celebrated life in bright colors, demonstrating joy in physical attractiveness." But plantation slaves had to concern themselves more with basic warmth.

Slave cabins were sparse in their furnishings. An inventory of one in Henrico County, Virginia, in 1697 shows "several chairs and a bed, an iron kettle weighing fifteen pounds, a brass kettle, an iron pot, a pair of pot racks, a pot hook, a frying-pan, and a beer barrel." Slaves probably had been in the cabin for some time. It was common for slaves to start or move with little more than a single iron pot and one frying pan. Slaves were not without resources, however. They could purchase or barter for household items, and as the eighteenth century passed, more cabins contained tables, linens, chamber pots, and a means of interior lighting.

What slaves ate varied greatly from one farm or plantation to another, depending on the produce of the region and the ideas of the master. Most colonial slaves seem to have existed on a basic core of meat and meal with some supplements. This was sufficient in quantity but lacking in quality. Advertisements for runaway slaves are full of references to physical problems associated with nutritional deficiencies: bad teeth, crooked legs, knocked knees, eye problems, poor posture, jaundiced or splotchy skin.

The idea that slaves existed on a "hog and hominy" routine is fairly sound. Most masters allowed a weekly ration of cornmeal—a peck for each slave was standard, or about a pound a day—and pork, three pounds "clear of bone" on average. There were regional variations and additions. African Americans in the southern low country ate rice, but they still consumed more corn; those in the Chesapeake in later years had greater access to wheat flour, from which they baked biscuits. Adult African Americans did not drink milk because of their genetic intolerance for lactose, and they ate little beef because it did not preserve well. Few slaves in colonial times supplemented their diets with peas, beans, sweet potatoes, or greens, as they may have done in the cotton South of later times. Most masters allowed slaves to raise produce, poultry, and pigs, but many did so to barter for tobacco, alcohol, or better clothes for Sundays and holidays rather than to improve their diets with fruits, vegetables, and more meat. The most popular (and dietarily useful) supplements were fish and game, the former important especially for persons in the low country and around New England ports.

Kenneth F. Kiple and Virginia Himmelsteib King in *Another Dimension of the Black Diaspora: Diet, Disease, and Racism* (1981) show that blacks had two major difficulties relating to diet and nutrition. Over centuries they had become adapted for survival in the African tropics, so once removed from the specialized environment they faced particular nutritional requirements that they could not meet easily in the British mainland colonies of North America. But regardless of their special needs, the diet they received in America, if sufficient in bulk, was not entirely sufficient in balance. Under such circumstances blacks in colonial America lived a kind of nutritional nightmare. The majority of slaves received insufficient protein of good quality and not enough of the vitamin B complex, vitamins C and D, and calcium and iron to meet their needs. The results included a rate of African American child mortality much higher than whites, development of personality disorders now recognized as associated with malnutrition, and a host of ailments and diseases in the slave population—the "Negro diseases" was what masters called them— that were largely foreign to whites. Among the debilitating and often fatal diseases particular to African Americans were rickets, pica (often referred to as "dirt-eating"), hookworm, and pellagra ("black tongue"). Of course, malnutrition often made slaves more susceptible to common diseases and made them vulnerable to secondary infections when they acquired a common ailment.

Given the nature of medical treatment in colonial times,

which included the letting of blood, application of leeches, administration of harsh purgatives, and lancing with unsterilized instruments, slaves who were unwell frequently were better off when masters did not summon professional medical advice. Blacks maintained their own medical system in the form of plantation or neighborhood "root doctors," who combined knowledge of herbal remedies with ritual skills to devise therapeutics for many of the slaves' ills. Actually, folk medical practitioners in Africa long had been adept at finding plants with medicinal properties and matching them to diseases. Also, the psychological benefit of believing in the healer, as African Americans seemed to do in their "root doctors," may have been as important as the medication in this early form of holistic medicine.

Closely tied to black medical treatment was another group of practices important to black folk culture that included magic, sorcery, and witchcraft. Belief in manipulation of spirits and in individuals who had special powers to use the spiritual realm to work magic for good and evil was widespread in western Africa where it moved beyond the religious and into the secular world. Africans brought such traditions to colonial America and melded them into a body of beliefs and practices sometimes called "voodoo" or slave magic. Most sizable groups of African Americans had one or more individuals, "conjurers" or "witch doctors," who worked their magic to help or harm people as required. One of the most frequently used magical practices was the wearing of amulets or talismans to protect from illness or harm. Blacks visited conjurers to find ways to get even with evil overseers or cruel masters, or to "give the mis'ries" to fellow slaves who had done misdeeds. Individuals in the African American community practiced divining, which included discovering lost property and telling the future. Belief in ghosts was common. It is important to note that in colonial America such African American folk beliefs were close to those of whites of the time and place. New England slaves feared witches nearly as much as whites did, and many were the white Yankees who visited noted black mediums for protection against ghosts or witches or to be healed of some affliction.

Considerable African influence was evident in black forms of music and dance. African technology went into the making and playing of a host of stringed instruments, certain fiddles, tambourines, flutes, xylophones, and drums. Blacks played these instruments in times of joy and sorrow; they sang together while hoeing crops, grinding corn, or rowing boats, and they joined together on moonlit nights to sing "sweet chants." Disgruntled slaves in the 1770s met among themselves to play African gourd-guitars and sing about what John Lovell, Jr. (*Black Song: The Forge and the Flame*, 1972) describes as "the usage they have received from their Masters and Mistresses in a very satirical style and manner." Folk narratives merged with song to provide instruction to children while entertaining them. Storytelling could be amusing or raunchy, depending on the audience. Dancing was a major way of celebrating. On African American holidays in New England, recalled Jane Shelton, groups of women "shuffled and tripped to the sound of the fiddle." African-style ring dances were popular, and some dances were raucous, noisy affairs that whites neither understood nor appreciated. Thomas Hazard seemed not to care for the dancing style of the Rhode Island slave Sam, "who had a way of his own of fetching a terrific screech like a catamount, and then dashing forward to the middle of the floor." Likewise, Pierre de Laussat wrote that slaves in South Carolina celebrated the Christmas holiday in dance by "distorting their frame in the most unnatural figures and emitting the most hideous noises." Not all neighbors of blacks appreciated their dances a great deal more. When a considerable number of African Americans persisted in gathering at William Grimes's "upper room" in New Bedford, Connecticut, dancing late into the night, Grimes's neighbors complained until his landlord revoked his lease.

African Americans knew how to enjoy a holiday or an evening away from work. Low-country slaves enjoyed boat races; blacks in Charleston liked to drink and play dice; New England blacks played "paw paw," a gambling game that became popular with blacks and whites in northern port towns. The biggest single celebration in colonial African American culture was Election Day in New England, when slaves took a holiday to elect their own "kings" and "governors" and to satirize white society. Free of normal restraints, slaves dressed elaborately for the holiday and celebrated with parades and "inaugural" parties. The officers elected became important personages in the black community.

The idea that acculturation in colonial America moved in a single direction—from Anglo-Americans to African Americans or Native Americans without spreading in reverse—is one that treats culture narrowly and does not hold up to careful examination of evidence. Not until the last few years have historians begun to realize how much African Americans have influenced important aspects of Euro-American culture. Most recently, Sobel has shown the extent of the interdependence of Anglo-Virginian and Afro-Virginian subcultures in colonial times. The two groups from different preindustrial worlds shared many of the same values and held many of the same ideas—especially in their thoughts of time, space, world view, causality, family ties, and death and the afterlife. In this environment, Sobel writes, Africans had considerable influence in the shaping of Euro-American culture. Until now, historians have been unaware of the widespread sharing of values between blacks and whites in the colonial years largely because of their sources. White people, who kept most of the records historians must rely on, simply failed to realize how much black thoughts and values changed their own ways of doing things and looking at the world.

# CHAPTER FOUR

# African Americans in the Revolutionary Era

The American Revolution was full of contradictions for African Americans. The clearest contradiction involved slavery and the ideology the Founding Fathers used to justify breaking with England. A third of the men who signed the document declaring their right to independent nationhood on the self-evident truth that all men are created equal owned other humans. In addition, the nation these men would create—the one that would secure the blessings of liberty to themselves and their posterity—was one whose social and economic fabric was woven with the thread of black slavery, whose population included half a million African American slaves, and whose wealthiest southerners would not consider joining a union of states without a clear recognition of their right to own others.

But the contradictions involved more than slavery and Revolutionary ideology. Among the results of the Revolution were paradoxical changes in African American society and culture. The Revolution made it possible for some blacks to gain their freedom. It led to the ending of slavery in the states north of Maryland and considerable manumission in the Upper South, and it gave even more African Americans the idea that freedom was not merely something good to obtain, but something one had a right to expect. However, white sons of the Revolution began circumscribing that freedom soon after numerous blacks had gained it. North and South, they cut away at African American rights, privileges, and opportunities, so that men and women who no longer were slaves remained separated and ostracized from the rest of American society. Also, for those thousands who remained in bondage and for the many thousands who would be slaves over the next eighty years, the Revolution made freedom more difficult to obtain. Slavery in the states south of Maryland grew in size and strength. Southern slaveholders became all the more convinced that the institution was necessary for their economic survival. And American independence entrenched slavery into the laws of the new land. Without mentioning slavery, the Constitution made the institution legitimate and gave slaveholders greater means to protect and defend their human property. In legitimizing slavery and strengthening the hold of slave owners, founders of the new nation set the stage for the enormous expansion of slavery into what would become the Cotton South—the open and newly acquired lands to the south and west early in the nineteenth century.

Yet most important for blacks in America over the long term, and probably most ironic, the Revolution brought a broadening and strengthening of the hierarchal order to American race relations. Although most English colonists held strong feelings about race before the Revolution, they did not need to use race so centrally to justify enslaving other human beings. Once Revolutionary theory made all persons free and equal with God-given inalienable rights, many who spoke the new ideals had cause to further entrench their racist feelings. They could rationalize slavery only by recognizing African Americans as a lower order, short on morals, long on muscle, quick to pilfer, slow to move, and hard to work. They could remain above the new and rapidly growing body of free blacks they despised only by using the same rationale. This affected all African Americans and laid the foundation for a stronger and more pervasive racist ideology that would plague the country from the time the Revolution had run its course until the present day.

## Slavery and Ideology

Westerners had long been in conflict over the existence of slavery in their society. Within the eighteenth-century body of thought we know of as the Enlightenment, strong intellectual forces emerged that worked against chattel slavery. Based initially on religious principles, and then bolstered by philanthropic tendencies accompanying the early growth of capitalism, antislavery sentiment arose in continental Europe and spread to England. By the time of the American Revolution, regardless of what else was going on, Western intellectuals and philosophers were reading and thinking and acting in a world that was debating slavery.

It was not as if there had been no opposition to slavery among British colonists on the North American mainland before 1750. To a few seventeenth-century Americans, human bondage had always been immoral and unchristian, and the number of opponents to slavery grew with the size of the slave population. A handful of New England Puritans and a few Scots and Salzburgers in Georgia spoke against slavery in the eighteenth century, but those who took the lead in expressing antislavery sentiment were members of the Society of Friends—the Quakers. Quakers were an anomaly because many of them made profits from the slave trade and owned slaves themselves. Not until the 1760s, when the supply of indentured servants increased and the supply of slaves decreased, did Philadelphia Quakers, for instance, begin following the antislavery principles they expressed formally in their yearly meetings. Nevertheless, as David Brion Davis writes in *The Problem of Slavery in Western Culture* (1966), "It would be difficult to exaggerate the central role Quakers played in initiating and sustaining the first antislavery movements." Some of them spoke out early. At a Friends meeting in Germantown, Pennsylvania, in 1688, a group of Quakers drafted a formal protest against slavery and "the traffic of men-body." In 1711 the Society of Friends in Rhode Island rid itself of a member who was mistreating a slave. By the middle of the eighteenth century the English-speaking world was becoming increasingly aware of the official Quaker antipathy for slavery. Under the leadership of such persons as John Woolman and Anthony Benezet, Quakers were pressing for disowning members of the Society who continued to hold slaves. If the early Quaker efforts were, as Donald L. Robinson argues in *Slavery and the Struggle for American Politics, 1765–1820* (1971), "like fireflies in the night," at least by the time of the Seven Years' War, Quakers had launched a frontal attack on the slave trade and had brought the broader ideas of antislavery thinking before the educated public, where they were ripe for debate. The tensions that grew between England and her mainland colonies after the Seven Years' War thus simultaneously raised arguments against and brought out rationalization of slavery, at the same time they were prompting colonists to question existing mercantile practices and to dwell on ways in which their political and economic lives could be better.

Many of the men who provided the ideology of the American Revolution considered themselves scions of the Enlightenment. Their faith in Man's limitless creative intelligence and rational, benevolent behavior brought them to apply their minds to creating a new order. No more oppression from religious zealots or tyrannous monarchs, no more misery or deprivation for the people in their society. The new order would provide persons of all classes the freedom to seek happiness and to unleash their talents on their natural circumstances for the benefit of all. The result would be what the rational, benevolent Creator intended.

Of course, it was an ideology into which slavery did not fit, and the American patriots knew it. Like despotism, slavery was a vestige of the Old World, a violation of rights. By being born human, people had rights to freedom, to gain from their work, to improve their lives as they wished. Skin color was not supposed to matter.

Much of this kind of thinking was in the mind of young Thomas Jefferson when he wrote the document that would justify the colonists' political break with England. Jefferson even blamed the English monarch for the slave trade and colonial slavery in the first draft of the Declaration of Independence. Members of the Continental Congress excised those portions because of the absurdity of blaming George III for what Rhode Island merchants and Virginia planters had been getting rich from for scores of years. However, slavery seemed to be doomed with the Declaration's first paragraph. All men were created equal; their God-given, unalienable rights included life, liberty, and the pursuit of happiness; governments were created to secure these rights. Nowhere did it limit application of this heady language.

But the new republic did not end slavery. It perpetuated the institution for the better part of another century. Why this happened and how the signers of the Declaration and framers of the Constitution (which put ideals into policy) could justify slavery as they were asserting the natural right of freedom for all are questions historians have grappled with for some time.

Jefferson easily becomes a symbol of the Revolutionary paradox and thus the focus of much of the questioning. Because he penned the words of the Declaration of Independence and espoused most eloquently its ideals, he stands out among those "enlightened" men who waged the rebellion and put together the new nation. Jefferson spoke often of wanting to end slavery in the spirit of the French *philosophes* he admired. Many have asked why the framer of the Declaration, the future president, and the slave owner never put into action his libertarian ideals, even with his own slaves. Answers have varied. One turns on the practical argument. In addition to being one of the most respected men in colonial America, Jefferson owned over two hundred slaves. They built his beloved Monticello and made it run. Jefferson also was one of Virginia's wealthiest citizens. He recognized that his economic position and political status were tied to a slave system. He knew the system was growing; demand for slaves was increasing steadily, values of human property were rising. Ending slavery would have meant political, social, and economic suicide for Jefferson and wealthy slave owners like him.

Another answer is based on Jefferson's deep-seated feelings of dislike for blacks. Today we would speak of his racism. Jefferson probably did not realize the strength and character of his racist feelings. In his *Notes on Virginia* (1785), which he intended for European intellectuals, Jefferson wrote from "scientific observation" of blacks' laziness and slowness, their inability to reason, their lack of imagination, and their unsightly appearance compounded by "wooly hair" and an "ungainly" physique. If Jefferson truly joined others of the Enlightenment in wanting to end chattel slavery, as he often wrote, his commitment to do so was theoretical and not real. He did not want to live with black persons as his equals in a free society. Racial prejudice joined with economic necessity, as he saw it, to keep him from putting theory into practice.

A third answer goes beyond Jefferson and has to do with proslavery sentiment among whites in at least part of the British North American mainland. White Virginians seemed to share Jefferson's dislike for blacks, but not so many held his expressed concern for slaves as humans. After all, Jefferson was one of the most enlightened members of American society—schooled at William and Mary, thoroughly read in history and philosophy, by thirty well versed in current libertarian ideas. Most of the rest of American society was different. In 1784 and 1785 over twelve hundred people signed petitions to the Virginia General Assembly opposing a 1782 Virginia law that simply allowed masters to free their slaves without legislative approval. The signers based their proslavery arguments on scripture and the right to private property that the Revolution affirmed. They were more representative of white southern colonists than the man who wrote the Declaration of Independence.

Important to remember, too, is that the fragile coalition of diverse economic and social groups that joined forces against England did so to wage a political revolution. What held the coalition together was agreement on wanting to rid themselves of English control. It was to justify independence that they agreed on the application of Enlightenment theory. But the small farmers and urban artisans, the northern capitalists and southern planters agreed on little else—indeed, the coalition broke apart before the newborn United States of America was past toddling—and they clearly did not agree on whether the new nation should proceed with or against slavery.

So in spite of the lofty ideals, the Revolution failed to eradicate slavery from the nation that replaced British rule over the North American mainland. But in raising the issues of freedom and human dignity the Revolution brought change of different shape and order to all parts of American society. For blacks in the northern states and for growing numbers in the Upper South this change meant becoming free persons. For those in the Lower South it meant greater personal independence, but within a slave system that was growing and becoming more deeply entrenched. And the arguments for freedom and the growing presence of free blacks led toward a hardening of racial lines and movement toward a system in which all African Americans, slave or free, would be regarded as members of a despised lower caste.

## Freedom for Some

The history of African Americans in the English North American mainland colonies for the century between 1670 and the outbreak of the American Revolution is a story of persons in bondage. In most places in North America there simply were no blacks who were not slaves. Good population figures do not exist for the colonies, but it seems that before 1770 free blacks made up only about 5 percent of the colonial African American population. Nearly all were in northern colonies, where they lived largely without influence in white society.

Many of the free blacks in pre-Revolutionary America were children of black-white marriages. A few had physical disabilities or were simply too old to be useful slaves.

From the time of the codification of slavery a century earlier, whites steadily had been reducing the liberties of those few free African Americans in their midst. In various places blacks' political rights were nonexistent and they were ostracized socially. Through most of the eighteenth century individual Virginians could manumit their slaves only with permission of the state assembly. Whites in southern colonies were especially blunt in expressing their views on free blacks. The governor of Virginia in 1723 asserted whites should place "a perpetual Brand upon Free-Negroes & Mulattos by excluding them from the great Priviledge of a Freeman," in order to "make the free-Negroes sensible that a distinction ought to be made between their offspring and the Descendants of an Englishman, with whom they never were to be Accounted Equal."

Neither Virginia's governor nor other southern whites— nor northern whites, for that matter—needed to worry about free blacks before 1770, but the Revolution altered the situation for all. The slave system of the nonplantation North did not last in the milieu of Revolutionary America. In rural areas it was not a strong institution by the middle of the eighteenth century. Landholders were dividing large estates that slaves had worked into small farms. Owners of more than a few slaves were having difficulty finding employment for their bondsmen through winter months. Persons not fond of African Americans anyway began questioning the necessity of bondage and, thus, of a black presence in the colonies.

Then the war came. A few owners manumitted slaves on condition they enlist in colonial militia units, and some of these northern blacks participated in the earliest skirmishes of the war. Benjamin Quarles in *The Negro in the American Revolution* (1961) names a dozen African Americans who fought with the other "minutemen" at Lexington and Concord, and he cites a December 1775 petition of fourteen Massachusetts officers to the General Court, stating "that a negro called Salem

Poor, of Col. Frye's regiment, Capt. Ames' company, in the late battle at Charlestown [Bunker Hill], behaved like an experienced officer, as well as an excellent soldier."

The fear that southern whites harbored at the prospect of arming blacks led to prohibitions on black recruitment, but not for long. By 1777, when Congress fixed troop quotas for each state and legislatures began offering bounties for enlistment, free blacks and slaves sent to serve for their masters began filtering into recruitment stations. By 1781 several states were ready to grant freedom to the slave and a bounty to the master for the slaves' three-year enlistment.

Many northern slaves ended their bondage by siding with the British, too. In the coastal cities to which British forces clung tenaciously, blacks served as auxiliaries on the promise of freedom. They worked as teamsters, carried messages, prepared food, and cleaned rubbish in New York and Philadelphia. At war's end British officers refused to turn slaves over to patriot forces. When they evacuated New York in 1783 the British took with them three thousand slaves, many of whom ended up as free residents of Canada or England.

The Revolution was a fertile medium for the growing moral opposition to slavery in the northern colonies. Antislavery forces had been active on the local level in New England since the 1750s. The Quaker campaign was strongest in Pennsylvania, and in Massachusetts and New Hampshire blacks petitioned for freedom and land. Efforts paid off by the late 1770s when states began writing constitutions that contained the Revolution's humanitarian ideals. Vermont was first to spell these out: "No male person ought to be holden by law to serve any person as a servant, slave, or apprentice after he arrives to the age of twenty-one years, nor female in like manner after she arrives to the age of eighteen years."

Meanwhile, dozens of test cases pecked away at the constitutionality of slavery in Massachusetts. As they did, slaves began leaving their masters, feeling certain that courts would not support their return. By 1783, when Massachusetts's Supreme Judicial Court, in the celebrated *Commonwealth* v. *Jen-*

*nison* case, found that the clause of the state's 1780 constitution declaring "all men are born free and equal" applied indeed to all, slavery in Massachusetts was on its last legs.

Elsewhere in the North abolition moved more slowly. Policies of gradual abolition ensured the Revolutionary generation its labor supply and enabled whites to keep African Americans in service until they could replace them with inexpensive white workers. The Pennsylvania General Assembly passed a gradual abolition law in 1780; Connecticut and Rhode Island did the same in 1784. New York and New Jersey, where Hudson River farmers dug in their heels on the issue, were slow to follow. Each passed its own gradual abolition bill, New York in 1799 and New Jersey in 1804, so slavery lingered for several decades. New York remained the last northern bastion of the institution with nearly twenty thousand slaves in 1800. These numbers declined through the next two decades, however, and for all practical purposes slavery ceased to exist in the northern states by the end of the first quarter of the nineteenth century.

One should not get the idea that abolition was smooth and easy in the North. Northern masters knew the value of their property—slaves brought good prices right up to the end as speculation dominated trading—and they fought abolition strongly. But economic conditions in the North helped abolition sentiment spread. Basic to the issue was that the northern economy did not have to have slavery, especially with the increasing number of inexpensive white laborers entering the country. Those who did not own slaves feared the advantages of people who did; white workers resented having to compete with slave labor. Both groups soon favored abolition. So it turned out to be easier to apply the humanitarian ideology of the Revolution to all people in places where universal freedom did not ravage the economy and even seemed to open the marketplace to fairer competition.

Many of the forces that affected African Americans in other areas of the land during Revolutionary times seemed to have been magnified for blacks in the Chesapeake. Perhaps this was because the region was the heart of the mainland slave society, just as it was the seedbed of rebellion and revolutionary ideology. Talk of abolition and acts of manumission had greater implications for whites who were so dependent on a system of human bondage. For blacks, the lure of freedom, which seemed closer and more real than in the Lower South, prompted men and women to take bolder action for their cause.

Virginia planters recognized their vulnerable position early on. Late in 1774, not long before British naval officers in Norfolk Harbor began taking aboard runaway slaves, a young James Madison wrote to a friend in Philadelphia:

If America and Britain should come to a hostile rupture I am afraid an Insurrection among the slaves may and will be promoted. In one of our Counties lately a few of those unhappy wretches met together and chose a leader who was to conduct them when the English troops should arrive—which they foolishly thought would be very soon and that by revolting to them they should be rewarded with their freedom. Their intentions were soon discovered and the proper precautions taken to prevent the Infection. It is prudent such attempts should be concealed as well as suppressed.

Through the summer of 1775, slaves calculated and threatened armed revolt in every southern colony. Then, as Madison feared, in November the colony's British governor, John Murray, fourth Earl of Dunmore, who was fighting Virginia's provisional government for control of the colony, offered freedom to slaves and servants who would join the British and bear arms against the rebellious colonists. In less than a year perhaps a thousand slaves made off to Dunmore's vessels in Chesapeake Bay. He would likely have gotten more had not a smallpox epidemic among the refugees discouraged others who thought of following. The governor was able to use some fugitives in the December 1775 British defeat at Great Bridge; then over part of the next year he sent small bands of armed blacks on boats and barges to forage and plunder Tidewater plantations, luring or forcing away more slaves.

After Dunmore's expulsion from a land base, British armies and privateers struck from the water at the plantation district between the James and York rivers, stealing livestock, tobacco, and slaves. When heavier fighting came to the region, British armies in Virginia and North Carolina took in runaways. In 1779 General Henry Clinton, British commander in chief, issued his Phillipsburg Proclamation, promising "to every Negro who shall desert the Rebel Standard, full security to follow within these lines, any Occupation which he shall think proper." More African Americans heeded the call. Alarmed members of the Virginia Convention quickly instituted measures to keep their labor force intact. They authorized summary punishment of runaways, sanctioned transportation and sale of recaptives to the West Indies, and sentenced others to incarceration with the hardest labor. Still, the African Americans kept running. Over the course of the fighting five thousand Chesapeake men and women in bondage found their way to the British forces. Many more learned of the promise of freedom, and their lives would never again be the same.

Unfortunately for the runaways, once cast with the British their lot seldom improved. Neither Dunmore, who never freed his own slaves, nor British army officers nor privateers were advocates of emancipation. The British army was interested in undermining the loyalists' economic base, and getting military laborers for its campaigns in North America or recruits for service in the West Indies. Black "spoils of war" ended up victims of army priorities. Worked long hours in hot weather constructing earthworks, digging and filling latrines, burying garbage, and generally doing labor no one else cared to perform (to save British soldiers for battle, officers argued), the poorly fed, clothed, and quartered African Americans suffered. Bouts of dysentery swept through their ranks, and because officers confined inoculation to white troops, smallpox epidemics hit blacks frequently. They died at alarming rates. Those who survived faced transport to East Florida, the British West Indies, or Nova Scotia, where life in slavery or freedom would be hard.

But fleeing to join the British was not the only way African Americans in the Upper South gained freedom. In the years immediately following the fighting, a new, steadily growing group of free blacks appeared in Maryland and Virginia. They were darker skinned and in much greater number than any who preceded them. Fighting on the side of the patriots, especially as substitutes for their masters, brought freedom to some slaves in the Upper South. Wartime chaos helped slaves run away too, and these fugitives found their way to Maryland or Virginia cities and worked hard at blending into the lowest urban class. Then, throughout the 1770s and 1780s, abolition sentiment, abetted by a sense of egalitarianism from the evangelical revival movement that continued to sweep the South, had effects. As Methodist and Baptist ministers chastised their congregations about slaveholding, guilt-ridden masters began freeing slaves or letting them accumulate property and purchase their freedom. In some places laws barring manumission fell to repeal.

With open manumission and talk of freedom at war's end, pressures increased. More fugitives headed north toward freedom, sometimes with assistance but largely unaided, beginning a trend that would continue and grow over the next seventy-five years. Although patrols increased, flight from slavery was easier now. With more free blacks in circulation and with light skin no longer a requirement for free status, runaways could avoid detection by blending into the free African American society. This was especially true in urban areas of the Upper South.

Once secure in their freedom, blacks worked to free their relatives. Some with good jobs saved for years to purchase kinsmen. John Hope Franklin in *The Free Negro in North Carolina, 1790–1860* (1943) writes of the case of John C. Stanley, a New Bern, North Carolina farmer and barber of extraordinary success since gaining his freedom in 1798. Between 1805 and 1818 Stanley purchased and freed his wife and two children, his wife's brother, and nineteen other African Americans in slavery. Some free blacks, unable to buy their loved ones, took other action. Enough free blacks assisted kinsmen in running away that wise masters kept tabs on their slaves' free relatives and thus knew where to look first for their fugitives.

Freedom did not bloom equally across the southern states. South Carolina and Georgia masters prohibited enlistment of blacks in the militia and freed only a tiny number of slaves. In fact, fears of any hint of a conspiracy that would lead to emancipation caused southern whites to react, sometimes with little respect for the law or humanity. Peter H. Wood describes the fate of Thomas Jeremiah in *The Southern Experience in the American Revolution*, edited by Jeffrey J. Crow and Larry E. Tise (1978). In the summer of 1775, Jeremiah, a valuable free black harbor pilot in Charleston, was accused, on questionable evidence, of collecting guns and urging other blacks to ready themselves "to fight against the Inhabitants of the Province." He was detained for two months and then, when fears heightened, was summarily brought to trial ("if such a process deserves the name," admitted South Carolina Governor Lord William Campbell), convicted, and shortly thereafter "hanged and then burned to ashes."

The farther south one went, the fewer slaves were able to run away and gain freedom without escaping the bounds of the new nation. In 1790, South Carolina had fewer than two thousand free blacks, mostly around Charleston. Georgia had four hundred. At the beginning of the nineteenth century the two states held only 7 percent of the free African American population of the South.

It was in northern Virginia and Maryland where manumission occurred most frequently and where slaves escaped without rapid detection. Thus, in this region the ranks of free blacks swelled steadily. By 1790 there were thirty thousand African Americans living in freedom in the upper South—a larger number than in the northern states—and over the next decade that number would double. The presence of such a body of African Americans outside the controls of the slave system would cause white society considerable anxiety and would consequently be a factor in bringing change to the Chesapeake's black society.

## Changing African American Society

Up and down the Atlantic Coast and inland toward the newly opening backcountry, the Revolution altered the lives of African Americans. North of Maryland, blacks experienced a gradual expansion of freedoms as slavery there died its slow death. In South Carolina and Georgia, slaves achieved greater independence, but it was independence within a slave system that was growing rapidly and becoming even more entrenched in white society. Blacks in the Chesapeake enjoyed greater freedom, too, with the rapid appearance and growth of the free black population and with more liberties in slavery, but this occurred against a backdrop of growing commitment to slavery through the southern parts of the region. And the geographical parameters of black life in bondage were spreading through the period, for out on the Virginia and Carolina frontiers a new slave society was forming, with implications for further expansion of the institution.

So through the last decades of the eighteenth century, black society continued to evolve differently in various sections of the country. There was even growing diversity within regions. But, as the group of essays shows in *Slavery and Freedom in the Age of the American Revolution* (1983), edited by Ronald Hoffman and Ira Berlin, across the growing diversity of black living conditions and life-styles one could detect the beginnings of a single, broad, distinctly African American society.

The transition from servitude to freedom in the North was surprisingly difficult. The timing of abolition, which varied by decades among the northern states, affected how slaves made the transition. So did regional demographic patterns, economic conditions, and white attitudes.

The popular image of African Americans learning of their freedom, usually through a statement from a sad master, and immediately casting off toward new lives appeals to romantic notions, but probably is inaccurate. Ties to "home," however connected with bondage "home" may have been, were strong, and there were practical considerations before one could hie for the city or even the farm down the road. First was livelihood. Freed slaves had to care for themselves, which usually meant they had to enter into arrangements of wage labor. Many went to work right away where they lived, and extrication from the master's household turned out to be a slow process. Between one-half and two-thirds of the men and women freed in the North were able to leave their masters within a few years of abolition, but for a third or more ties were firm, the security was real, and leaving for good took longer.

Even for those who remained in or around the master's residence, the end of slavery brought African Americans a clear sense of being different people, no longer bound by the personalities or rules of their masters. Studies of slave naming patterns in northern states show how slaves broke with their past almost immediately upon becoming free by ceasing to use the old, derisive first names their masters had given them— the classical Pompey or Caesar, the African day names of Cuffee or Quash, or such place names as York or Jamaica. They moved away also from the surnames of their masters. The names they chose, however, with many biblical first names and more English first and last names, suggest how far acculturation had come for African Americans in the North.

Many blacks in rural areas found seasonal wage labor on small farms near where they lived, but many also moved toward the greater opportunities offered in the northern coastal cities. African American populations of Boston, New York, and Philadelphia soared with the ending of the war. New York's population of free blacks lagged behind the others because of the continuing existence of a large slave population. Philadelphia attracted newly freed blacks and runaways from

Maryland and Virginia to the extent that between 1780 and 1800, while the city's white population was doubling, its African American population was increasing sixfold.

Part of the lure of northern cities was economic opportunity. If the urban setting offered little room for advancement, it still held the possibility of sustaining oneself on a low level. More African American women moved to the city than men because jobs for domestics were always plentiful. Most men worked as day laborers, especially in the maritime industry, but urban blacks held positions as artisans and shopkeepers in about the same numbers as when slavery existed there.

The city also offered free blacks the advantage of living with others of their culture. Blacks living in small numbers in the northern countryside were isolated and thus targets for white hostility, which rose with the ending of slavery. But in the city, African Americans in good numbers lived near one another and soon black community institutions existed that provided them security. It was in the city that men and women could more easily find marriage partners and begin families; it was there they could join in worship, combine resources to educate their young, and come together for camaraderie and mutual support.

Freedom was surprisingly disruptive and hard on African American families. By 1770 most of black society in America had its basis in the family. Becoming free and moving away from the master's household disturbed the family's stability. In addition to normal problems associated with poverty, especially husbands and wives being too poor to live together, black families often experienced the unsettling circumstances of moving and resettling. It would take time to create stable family life in a new setting. Once extricated from white residences but not yet able to form their own nuclear households, poor blacks often combined with relatives or friends to establish separate residences. Taking in boarders helped pay expenses. Transition to a pattern of two-parent households took about a generation from abolition. Yet far from being the unstable, matrilocal institution that social scientists long portrayed, the postabolition African American family in the North became stable and autonomous soon after it appeared. Both parents lived at home and played important roles in the maintenance of the household.

In rural areas black residence patterns remained separate and varied, but in northern cities one could see by the 1780s the beginnings of a pattern of residential clustering and the formation of small but integral neighborhoods. Separate black churches appeared, initially as refuges from discrimination in white churches and as places where blacks could worship in the emotional fashion they preferred. Churches provided burial grounds, centers for common activities, and seedbeds for formation of benevolent and fraternal organizations. Congregations pooled their resources and started "African" schools for training their young.

Gary B. Nash in "Forging Freedom: The Emancipation Experience in the Northern Seaport Cities, 1775–1820" in *Slavery and Freedom in the Age of the American Revolution* shows how the continued existence of slavery in New York delayed development of community institutions. Obtaining freedom required the resources of those who were free. Then, once free, a generation passed before African Americans were able to move and become part of a neighborhood where people had a community of interests. But by the end of the Revolutionary era, the basis would be there for the growth of black social and community institutions that, by the early nineteenth century, would be the envy of poor whites in similar situations.

If the Revolution first brought questioning and then the demise of slavery in the North, it generally failed to cause whites in the country's southern extreme to reflect seriously on the rectitude of slave society. In fact, slavery in South Carolina and Georgia began a period of entrenchment and expansion just as the institution began to die in the northern states. The result by the end of the Revolutionary era would be the existence of a more powerful and viable southern institution, with prominent whites sure of slavery's necessity and, therefore, adamant about their right to own and forcibly work other humans. For the slaves, ironically, the same period brought still greater autonomy and, with a new wave of importation of Africans, a reinvigoration of the subculture that was more "African" than any other on the mainland.

Philip D. Morgan in "Black Society in the Lowcountry, 1760–1810" in *Slavery and Freedom in the Age of the American Revolution* argues that demographic and economic changes of the last half of the eighteenth century had considerable effect on the lives of African Americans and on the institution of slavery in South Carolina and Georgia. The natural increase of the slave population from about 1750; the growing size of low-country plantations, with increasing specialization of slave duties; the movement of rice cultivation to tidewater lands, which changed the kinds and amount of work black people performed; and the gradual opening of the backcountry to slavery, with overland importation of slaves, brought greater change to the lives of blacks in the Lower South than did the Revolution.

Not that the Revolution was not disruptive. British armies occupied Charleston and Savannah, and marauding groups of soldiers from both sides marched back and forth across low-country lands, foraging, plundering, and killing. Planters hustled their human property off, ahead of one or another army. Others just took care of themselves. Out of the disturbance came real hardship for many blacks, but also came the opportunity to flee. As in Virginia, African Americans in South Carolina were the victims of kidnapping and plundering, and epidemics swept off large numbers of them. Some, of course, simply made off and never returned.

Boston King, a slave of patriot Richard Waring living near Charleston through the late 1770s, exemplifies the difficulties the Revolution brought and the opportunities for a new life it provided. ("Memoirs of the Life of BOSTON KING, a Black Preacher," *The Methodist Magazine for the Year 1798*.) When the British captured Charleston in May 1780, King "determined to go to Charles-Town, and throw myself into the hands of the English." So many others did so at the same time that British troops were nearly overwhelmed. King recalled feeling "the happiness of liberty, of which I knew nothing before, altho' I was much grieved at first, to be obliged to leave my friends, and reside among strangers."

King's happiness soon was tempered, however, as he fell victim to the smallpox epidemic that was sweeping through the ranks of the African Americans in the city. He spent miserable days at a camp where the British army attempted to quarantine the sick fugitives. "We lay sometimes a whole day without any thing to eat or drink," he remembered, "but Providence sent a man, who belonged to the York volunteers whom I was acquainted with, to my relief. He brought me such things as I stood in need of; and by the blessing of the Lord I began to recover." Eventually, soldiers hauled him in a cart with twenty-five other invalids to a cottage, near a British hospital, where slowly he regained his health.

King then marched off with the army of General Cornwallis, serving as an orderly to a succession of British and loyalist officers. Somehow, he found himself with a unit of 250 British soldiers who were surrounded by a force of 1,600 patriots. On promise of a reward, King stole through the patriot lines and traveled twenty-four miles to a larger British force, taking word of his unit's plight. His reward turned out to be a few shillings. Soon back in Charleston, King joined the crew of a British man-of-war and sailed to New York. He was one of the three thousand blacks evacuated from New York in 1783 and taken to Nova Scotia.

By war's end, countless African Americans in South Carolina had died, disappeared, or gained their freedom like King. The colony's black population was reduced by about one-quarter—twenty-five thousand men and women. More Georgia slaves actually escaped through the period, seven thousand to British lines and untold numbers to Spanish lands or Indian territory to the south and west.

The war had long-term effects for the blacks who remained. British occupation and the chaos in the countryside left a void in control. South Carolina slaves did not run away in the numbers owners feared because of continual, more careful patrolling and because both sides in the war discouraged runaways. South Carolina's white leaders "received with horror" a Continental Congress proposal in 1779 to recruit slave soldiers, and British forces were hardly armies of liberation. Without resources to handle large numbers of dependents, and never having much desire to liberate enslaved African Americans anyway (since many loyalists were slave owners), the British army rationalized that the slaves were "ungovernable" and saw to it that they stayed put.

Out on the plantation, sometimes left alone for weeks or months at a time, African Americans carved out new, more liberal bounds for their activities. Black slave drivers, already powerful with the frequent absence of owners, became more involved in planning and management. Their authority reached new levels. Other slaves took on greater responsibilities, accumulated more property, and participated more in interplantation commerce and regional trade. Once the English left and the planters returned, it was practically impossible to return to the old, more restrictive ways of low-country plantation life.

Urban slaves expanded their parameters too. By 1770 many Charleston slaves had grown up in the open urban environment and were typical of city populations everywhere— more autonomous, more highly skilled, more ready to take advantage of opportunities, especially in trade. Between periods of loyalist and patriot control, African Americans assumed larger roles in supplying each side with provisions. They marketed their skills to the highest bidders. Slaves worked for the armies as spies, informants, and couriers. One Savannah slave, Quamino Dolley, guided British forces through a maze of swamps to surprise colonial forces from the rear, helping insure British capture of the city. Blacks from the region were especially good at foraging. They knew the plantations with the best livestock and provisions. When the British evacuated Charleston and Savannah in 1782, they took with them twelve thousand African Americans. Unfortunately, the destination for many of this number was the British West Indies, where apparently their would-be saviors sold them back into slavery.

The greater independence of all South Carolina and Georgia blacks allowed them to strengthen family ties and broaden their already strong, hybrid subculture. After the Revolution, more African American men and women on plantations were able to live with their families, which now extended over several generations, and owners showed more respect for the family units of their slaves. African American culture remained divided as before the Revolution, with urban slaves more acculturated and rural blacks clinging to African customs. The reinstitution of the slave trade after the war's end brought a final influx of African elements into low-country black culture and insured that it would continue to have strong African influences and be, as Morgan puts it, "in many ways disengaged from the white world."

Yet the end of the Revolutionary years saw low-country landowners believing more strongly than ever in the efficacy of the slave system and more willing and able to perpetuate that system. In the low country the idea that acquiring slaves was the way to prosperity flourished; nowhere in the new country was it more current. Soon after the end of hostilities, the economy of the low country boomed. Georgia first and then South Carolina reopened the Atlantic trade and rapidly imported enough Africans to replace losses from the war. They continued to import large numbers of Africans so that whites could move to the backcountry with their laborers. The power and wealth of southern landowners began increasing as the system of slave labor expanded to include the growing of new crops. The indigo market disappeared with the loss of the English market in the war years, but planters began growing a new crop, cotton, and that started spreading slowly inland after 1790. By 1800 slavery in the low country had new life. South Carolina and Georgia planters would be in good positions to take advantage of opportunities the expanding economy would offer them.

In Virginia and Maryland the Revolution brought even greater dislocation and change. Blacks and whites appeared on the move everywhere and to some the movement seemed to be turning society about. In Virginia there was westward movement toward the Blue Ridge. Some slave owners took their bondsmen out of reach of the fighting; others merely saw advantage in establishing upland farms on fertile new lands. Those who stayed recognized the heavily creole slave population would grow rapidly through natural increase. Slaves and land were available. As the market for tobacco fell with the war, Chesapeake planters turned to mixed farming. Although tidewater soils had lost fertility over the generations of tobacco growing, planters relied on increasing numbers of black workers to squeeze profits from the land.

Farmers in the Upper Chesapeake did not have the outlet of a western frontier. Planters in Maryland already had turned to producing cereal, which thrived on small farms with free labor, so slavery did not grow and expand as in the central and southern parts of Virginia. Slave prices fell in Maryland, and although the numbers of persons in bondage grew in the Upper Chesapeake for two decades after the war, the Revolution marked the beginning of the splitting of Chesapeake slave society. In Maryland and northernmost Virginia slavery would be less important for the economy and there would be a movement toward greater freedom. In the central and southern Virginia Piedmont and Tidewater the trend would be in the opposite direction. Slavery became more entrenched, the number of white slaveholders increased, and the African American population grew rapidly by natural increase as the nineteenth century approached.

Free blacks in the Chesapeake went through changes similar to those in the North. They found jobs, took new residences, changed names, reconstructed families or made new ones, and slowly developed the community institutions—schools, churches, benevolent societies—that helped ease the social transition, prepared people for life's problems, and provided individuals a communal identity.

It was common for some blacks in the Upper South to experience a decline in occupational status with freedom. Because white artisans feared free black competition, they were hostile to African Americans trying to practice trades. Furthermore, free blacks seldom had resources to purchase or even rent land, and when they did, whites were reluctant to sell or rent to them. Small numbers of free blacks overcame these obstacles and became successful farmers, professionals, shopkeepers, artisans, and showmen. They formed the seedbed of the southern African American elite that would appear in the first decades of the nineteenth century.

Those who were not so fortunate still found benefits in the southern economy, which was changing in America's early years. With tobacco declining and cereal production increasing, whites were leaving the Tidewater for opportunities in the newly opened lands to the west. Landowners needed to replace white tenants, and poor blacks saw farm tenancy as a step toward accumulating resources to buy land. Thus, with the exception of those in Baltimore or Fredericksburg, free African Americans in late-eighteenth-century Maryland and northern Virginia tended to live a rather isolated existence in the country, renting or working as tenants or hired laborers at grain farming.

The Revolutionary generation of free blacks in the Upper South did not try immediately to separate themselves from whites and their institutions. This is evident in black participation in white-dominated evangelical churches and, less commonly, in their joining with whites to establish integrated schools. Evangelical ministers welcomed all who accepted the Gospel, and they appealed to blacks with their emotional, participatory services. Blacks flocked to the Methodist and Baptist churches, and by the 1790s congregations of blacks and whites, although normally segregated, on occasion listened together to exhortations of African American preachers.

By late in the century, however, a movement of blacks to separate institutions was underway. Barred from some white churches and never full members of others, free blacks began taking control of their religious lives by forming "African" churches. These black churches spawned fraternal organizations and benevolent societies, and often developed auxiliary institutions for educating their young.

The most widely known example of this process was the work of Richard Allen in forming the Bethel African Methodist Episcopal Church in Philadelphia. Allen had been a slave in Delaware until 1777, when he purchased his freedom and, almost simultaneously, was converted to Methodism. He was already a successful preacher when he moved to Philadelphia in 1786 and became a leader of prayer meetings for fellow African Americans. He attended and sometimes preached at the integrated St. George Methodist Church until white officials spoke of segregating blacks who came to hear Allen's exhortations. When a church trustee interrupted Allen and several companions in prayer, pulling one from his knees and sending the group to the rear of the gallery for their "proper" place to pray, Allen led his flock elsewhere. Within a few years he would establish what would become the Bethel AME Church, and by 1799 Allen would be the church's first deacon.

Ministers like Allen were the focus of activity in the free African American community. They preached on Sundays, led social and religious gatherings on weeknights, and during the day served as schoolmasters. Their churches grew rapidly to become the heart of the free black society. The ministers became the community's leaders, and from their institutional bases they guided the long evolution of independent African American culture through the nineteenth century.

Neither the growing independence on the plantation nor the development of the free black community held the greatest implications for southern African Americans in 1790; it was the opening of new lands, the westward movement of slaves, and the early formation of expanded slave societies in new areas.

When the fighting of the Revolution was over, Americans quickly pushed Indians out and opened new lands on the western frontier. Availability of these lands brought adventure-some men in the 1780s and 1790s to migrate into Kentucky, Tennessee, and western Georgia and South Carolina. To perform the difficult process of clearing land for farms, they brought along slaves. There were enough slaves in the Chesapeake to meet the demands of western migrants, but not nearly enough in South Carolina and Georgia, where slave agriculture was booming and where many African Americans had run away or died during the war. Once Spain ceded much of modern Mississippi and Alabama to the United States in the Pinckney Treaty of 1795 and thus opened new lands to settlement, the southern states needed still more slaves. As a consequence, South Carolina and Georgia insisted on keeping open the Atlantic slave trade for two more decades. Between 1788 and 1808 the two states imported slaves at a greater rate than ever before into the North American mainland. Nearly one hundred thousand Africans entered Charleston, Savannah, and smaller ports along the low-country coast before Congress ended the traffic on January 1, 1808.

Western migration disrupted the already settled African American communities and slowed acculturation. Moving often forced slaves to separate from their families and relocate permanently to different parts of the country for new kinds of harder work. The proportion of southern slaves who had to face this separation grew steadily. In the Chesapeake it was one in twelve in the 1790s, one in ten in the 1800s, and as cotton production became increasingly important and Chesapeake slaves moved south and west, one in five in the 1810s. African slaves arriving in the low country around the turn of the century faced rapid sale and movement westward, where they mixed with creole slaves and began to acculturate out on the frontier. Black communities would have to form again, and it would take time. In Kentucky and Tennessee slaves had difficulty finding new marriage partners in spite of a balance between sexes. Living in groups of fewer than four on small farms, these workers did not have the contact with large numbers of fellow blacks that made community possible. Farther south, slaves lived on larger units, but the creole-African split kept them separated for a generation. Back in the Chesapeake, African American families weathered the disruption. Those who remained rebuilt networks of kinship and camaraderie. Now, however, they were aware of the threat of forced removal and of the continuing struggle it would be to maintain family and community ties.

By the end of the Revolution, ironic circumstances appeared in African American society. On the one hand there was the new, clear division between free blacks and those enslaved that was similar in many ways to the old split between Africans and creoles. But on the other was the first indication of broad unity across the breadth of all African American society. As always, regional variants of black society continued to evolve in their own fashion, and there remained obvious differences in black ways of life. No doubt it was difficult to recognize social commonalities between African Americans living in Philadelphia, for example, and Gullah slaves on low-country plantations. Also, the waning social and cultural split between Africans and slaves born in America lingered in the South Carolina and Georgia backcountry.

But beyond these divisions was a hint of the emergence of the broad African American cultural unity that would eventually prevail. Hardening racial attitudes of whites and their growing inclinations to separate and treat in discriminating fashion everyone of African descent, regardless of servile status, brought African Americans to recognize what they had in common. In addition to their African heritage and such unifying manifestations of culture as religious practice, close kinship ties, and general folkways, free blacks were not so long out of slavery and not welcome enough in white society to lose contact and identity with their cultural counterparts in bondage. As a result, as African American society continued to evolve— indeed, as free blacks in the North and Upper South proceeded to grasp what advantages they could find while southern blacks were becoming involved in a slave system of expanding scope and importance—it became more evident that their lots were cast together. By 1800, African Americans were part of a single

American society. Over the long run of the nineteenth century, what befell one group would come to affect the other.

## The Foundations of Caste

The debate over the origin of racism in America comes alive again with examination of the Revolutionary era. Before coming to America, the English had strong feelings about Africans; racism was important in establishment of black slavery in the British mainland colonies; and the existence of slavery in colonial times, with the required brutal punishments to make black men and women work as hard as their masters demanded, reinforced and even strengthened the racist sentiments and beliefs of white colonists. But race was not of over-riding importance through the colonial period—perhaps only because it did not need to be. The bodies of laws that governed slavery reflected the racial prejudices of the lawmakers, but few questioned society's right to design laws to regulate its lowest class of laborers. One did not have to justify slave codes with arguments of black inferiority. And through the middle of the eighteenth century, African Americans and white Americans continued to mix and share their values, their customs, and many aspects of their lives.

Developments that occurred through the time of the American Revolution changed all this. The debate over slavery on moral and religious grounds took on new meaning when colonists began discussing the position of slavery in their new, democratic society. If the country's existence rested on the doctrine of people having individual freedom, where did slavery fit? More convinced than ever of the necessity of slavery for their economic well-being and their elevated social status, southerners were on the spot. How could they subscribe to American principles and defend slave society? In devising answers they fell back on old racist assumptions that focused on the "nature and character" of blacks.

Southern white racism thus descended into the depths of the evil and absurd. Blacks were different, white southerners argued. They could not live in a free society as equals of white men because of their racial inferiority. They were different physically, as anyone could see. They had "wooly" hair, flat noses, and thick lips, and they had their own smell (Jefferson himself had made these points). They were of lower intelligence and lazy, making it impossible for them to compete in a free society; they were inclined toward crime, excessive drink, and boisterous behavior; and they had no compunction against lying. Most serious (southern men insisted), blacks were sexually depraved, the women promiscuous and the men rapists at heart. They argued that such people were dangerous in a free state. Society had to watch them closely and provide careful control. Keeping them in slavery, they reasoned, was the best way to do so.

As so often happens in such instances, southern whites took note of evidence that sustained them in their beliefs, and ignored things that did not bear out their racist notions. Some of what was happening in urban centers, where a free African American society was getting on its feet, seemed to support their thinking. Blacks in American cities were having expected difficulties. They were in jail or were wards of the community out of proportion to their numbers. Few thought of the lingering effects of slavery when considering these social ills. (Of course, southern whites had to ignore the highly skilled slaves all around them if they were to believe the problem was African Americans' base nature and general inability, but such were the workings of the racist mind.)

Compounding the problem was some of the crude social-scientific inquiry of Western intellectuals of the time. A common belief was that humans were at the top end of a long "chain of being" and whites were more advanced along the chain than blacks. Linnaeus's *Systema Naturae*, tenth edition (1758–59), a standard reference for educated persons of the late eighteenth century, identified variants of *homo sapiens* in physical and cultural terms. *Europaeus* was white, sanguine, and muscular with long, flowing hair and blue eyes; was gentle, acute, and inventive; was covered with close vestments and governed by laws. *Afer*, located below *Europaeus*

on Linnaeus's vertical chart, was black, phlegmatic, and re-
laxed, with black and frizzled hair, silky skin, flat nose, and
"tumid" lips. Black women were, in Linnaeus's view, "without shame"; their "Mammae lactate profusely." *Afer* was
crafty, indolent, and negligent; was self-anointed with grease;
was governed "by caprice." Those believing in human brotherhood had only Christian doctrine or Revolutionary principles on which to base their beliefs. It was difficult for anyone to disagree with the vehement arguments of slaveholders
when the southerners had "scientific evidence" to support
them.

It was in this context of a growing racist rationale for
enslaving blacks that the states sent representatives to Philadelphia to agree on a Constitution setting up a stronger union.
Northern states were beginning to dismantle slavery, and some
of their delegates thought abolition should be a natural, if gradually instituted result of the Revolution. But delegates from
the Lower South blocked the road. Increasingly as convinced
of their racist beliefs as they were of the necessity of slavery
for their survival, southern statesmen simply refused to join
a union that would not guarantee slave interests. The greatest
split among state delegates at the Constitutional Convention
was between those from North and South.

The Constitution that resulted rested on compromises between slaveholders and nonslaveholders, and was remarkable
for the words it left out. Delegates from South Carolina and
Georgia made known their opposition to any government that
might immediately restrict their ability to import slaves or
ignore human property in counting population for representation. They found northern delegates willing to compromise
on these issues for the sake of union—and for southern conces-
sions to federal authority in regulation of interstate and foreign
trade. So the final draft of the Constitution showed agreement
on prohibiting Congress from interfering with the importing
of slaves before 1808 and on counting three-fifths of all slaves
for apportioning taxes and representatives. Delegates came to

terms more easily on a clause requiring states to return fugitive slaves.

The Constitution neither authorized specifically the holding of humans in bondage nor mentioned the words *slave* or *slavery* in its entirety. It forbid Congress to prohibit importation of "such persons as the several states shall think proper to admit"; it added to the whole number of free persons "three-fifths of all other persons" for representation and taxation; and it required a state to deliver up on claim a "person held to service or labour" in another state. But the document did not have to sanction slavery or even refer to it by name to solidify the institution in southern society. The Constitution was a document that guaranteed individual rights to property above all, and as such it accommodated slavery because slaves were the property that, next to land, was most important to white southerners. The Constitution provided tacit recognition of slavery, it left to the states the authority to decide on the institution's fate, and it provided the power of the federal government to enforce the law and keep order. In so doing, it strengthened the hold slaveholders had on their bondsmen, and it made possible the steady extension of the institution across new southern and western lands as the nineteenth century unfolded.

With antislavery agitation spreading and with increasing numbers of free blacks in their presence, southern whites began, as Winthrop Jordan asserts in *White Over Black*, "hardening and polishing the structure of slavery." In parts of Virginia, proslavery petitions abounded. One, signed by 161 freeholders of the state's southside Lunenburg County, showed the animosity that fear wrought, as it predicted that general emancipation would result in

Want, Poverty, Distress & Ruin to the free Citizens; the Horrors of all the Rapes, Robberies, Murders, and Outrages, which an innuerable Host of unprincipled, unpropertied, vindictive, and remorseless Banditti are capable of perpetrating; Neglect, Famine and Death to the abandoned black infant and superannuated Parent; inevitable Bankruptcy to the Revenue; Desperation and revolt to the disappointed, oppressed Citizen; and sure and final ruin to this happy, free and flourishing Country.

Southern states curbed practices of hiring out slaves, according to a Maryland act, "to prevent the inconvenience arising from slaves being permitted to act as free." Steadily, they made private manumission more difficult to accomplish, and they moved even more in the direction of establishing slavery as the tightly guarded and restricted institution it would become in the Antebellum South.

The early manifestations of hardening racist ideas fell most directly not on slaves but on free blacks. For a short time after the war, when their numbers were small, free African Americans basked in the limelight of the Revolution. Even southern states wrote constitutions guaranteeing basic rights to all, and there was little thought of barring some free citizens from these rights. But as the group of free blacks in the Upper South grew, and as it included many who were not easily identified by their light skins, southern whites began a fear and loathing of African Americans not in bondage. Free blacks were dangerous to the institution of slavery, southern whites asserted. They could promote unrest and aid runaways and rebels. Even more threatening, by their very existence (heightened by any success they might attain), they undermined the racist justification for black slavery that was the crux of slaveholders' arguments for existence of the institution in the era of the "rights of man." No longer could whites allow free blacks a hint of equal treatment. Controlling the size of the free African American community became a priority for state legislatures. In the 1790s states began limiting and then banning African American immigration. Southern states encouraged free blacks to emigrate to middle and northern states, prompting some of the latter to enact laws prohibiting blacks entering for purposes of residence.

When states could not purge themselves of free blacks, they set about expropriating the new liberties Revolutionary constitutions provided them. African Americans had to register with state governments and in some cases provide security for good behavior. Authorities presumed blacks to be slaves until they proved otherwise, and requirements for free blacks waxed stringent the farther south one went. In North Carolina, for instance, all free blacks in urban areas had to register with the city government and wear a shoulder patch inscribed "FREE." States restricted intercounty mobility and made possible the binding over to white guardianship of young free African Americans. Some blacks soon found themselves having to pay special taxes, being refused enlistment in militias, and deprived of their rights to vote and bear arms.

Before the eighteenth century was over a clear tendency to separate the races was becoming evident. This was neither necessary nor possible on plantations and smaller farms, but in cities throughout the country whites moved to exclude all African Americans, free or slave, from social activities where whites were involved. In public facilities African Americans got separate, inferior accommodations. White churches either proscribed blacks or treated them as second-class members. Restaurants and taverns moved blacks to separate sections; clubs, fraternal organizations, and trade unions simply refused to admit them to membership. African Americans were not welcome in white schools or, in many cases, in white cemeteries. The issue was not slavery. It was race.

Such patterns of segregation seldom needed to be written into law. They entered into custom and became society's norms. These customs spread out of the South and across the free states through the first half of the nineteenth century. From the end of the colonial era, racist ideas and practices of separation would be part of American patterns of thought and modes of behavior for two more centuries of African American life.

# EPILOGUE

For African Americans there was nothing magic about the ending of the Revolution and the beginning of the new country. In most of the states that ratified the Constitution, slavery proceeded unchecked. Its death in the North would be a slow one, and in the South the institution would not be many years away from gaining new vitality. As the first Congress was working on Constitutional guarantees of what Representative James Madison called the "great rights of mankind," which included the Fifth Amendment assurance that no person was to "be deprived of life, liberty, or property without due process of law," New England merchants were beginning again to bring large numbers of captive Africans into southern ports. Also at that very time, southern planters were experimenting with varieties of cotton that they could produce to meet the demand of the expanding English textile industry. It would be only a few years before Eli Whitney's invention for separating cotton seeds from the lint would make feasible the widespread growing of a short-staple variety of the plant. Cotton production was then quick to spread. Once it began doing so, such events as the successful slave revolutions on Saint Domingue in the Caribbean or the prohibition of importing slaves into the United States, after January 1, 1808, could not check slavery's expansion in those states where cotton might grow.

What was important for African Americans about the ending of the colonial period, however, was that by then the major institutions and forces that would affect their lives and those of their descendants over the next two centuries were established or in motion. By 1790 the southern economy and society were so thoroughly bound up in slavery that its most prominent citizens opposed entering a union that threatened their right to own human beings. Adventuresome southern whites, who knew the way to get ahead was to obtain land and make it produce with slave labor, already were beginning to move westward with the African Americans they held in bondage, anticipating the movement of the cotton boom a generation later. To help recover from the Revolution and to service the expanding economy, southerners imported nearly one hundred thousand more African slaves between 1790 and 1808.

Yet by 1790, the sectional split among states that would lead to the Civil War and then to slavery's demise was evident. The libertarian ideals of the Revolution and the egalitarian spirit of the Great Awakening had served as catalysts for antislavery sentiment, and a movement toward abolition, although weak, was alive in the country. The Northwest Ordinance of 1787 already marked lands north of the Ohio River as free states for the union's future. Most of the arguments for and against slavery (and its extension into new territories) that statesmen would debate so vigorously in the 1840s and 1850s had been aired by the time the Founding Fathers signed the Constitution.

By the end of the eighteenth century black individuals had established their own modes of resistance to the institution that bound their lives, and they would continue to malinger, run away, or rebel as their situation made possible until slavery ended. Even afterward, when free blacks in the South found themselves bound to tenant farms on the same land their ancestors tilled as slaves, they would use some of the same means to resist. On into the twentieth century, running away—

after 1910 it occurred in such numbers that it was thought of as "migration" out of the South, to northern and western cities—remained a popular black reaction to oppressive conditions.

Moreover, the long period of black Americans' social and cultural evolution brought into existence by 1790 a stable, identifiable African American culture that encompassed the societies of free blacks as well as slaves. Their culture was anchored in the family and a community that had found the means to survive under difficult circumstances; it had different manifestations in the North, Upper South, and Lower South; its focus was on religion and the church; and American blacks had folkways and traditions all their own. When African Americans moved after 1790, their culture moved with them. Thus, a variation would constitute the culture of slaves in the antebellum South. As Genovese shows in *Roll, Jordan, Roll,* this culture, which continued to grow and change and move with American blacks from its earlier foundation, formed the basis for African American identity in a hostile world.

Late colonial demographic trends among African Americans even show the beginnings of population movements and settlement patterns that would be characteristic of free blacks before the Civil War and of all persons of African descent for the century afterward. A vague and gradual, but still noticeable, northward movement of black people began in the Revolutionary era, at least out of the Upper South toward the Middle states. As the body of free blacks increased in size, individuals and groups began moving toward urban areas, where jobs existed and African American communities provided more comfortable settings and group support. In the largest northern cities, Philadelphia and New York in particular, the seeds that would grow much later into African American neighborhoods, then black ghettos, were already in the soil by the close of the colonial period.

Finally, one does not have to look deeply into the American society of 1790 to see the roots of the racism that has since plagued the nation. Rigid, unreasonable racial prejudice was evident and spreading, and it was more than a southern phenomenon. Already by 1786 New Jersey had prohibited free blacks from entering the state. Other states would follow. Within two decades northern states began disfranchising blacks—President Jefferson signed a bill in 1802 excluding African Americans from voting in the nation's new capital—and as soon as blacks threatened to take white jobs, whites moved to deny skilled African Americans opportunities to practice their trades. Across the growing country, from bases where whites and blacks lived together, spread customary racial separation and along with it the discrimination, social ostracism, and exploitation that would persist and continue to evolve as they had through the colonial period.

Thus, the truly formative years of the black experience in America seem to have been the earliest ones. By the beginning of the nineteenth century the major forces already were in motion that would affect the way African Americans would live for the long period to follow.

# BIBLIOGRAPHICAL ESSAY

Study of the experience of African Americans from their African origins through the colonial era involves working in two distinct bodies of historical literature. To examine the African background and the slave trade one must consult work done largely by specialists in Africa or the South Atlantic zone, but to study the institution of slavery in the British mainland colonies one has to turn to the work of American historians who consider their study as part of a larger body that provides a history of the United States. Fortunately, both groups have been active over the past two decades, and what we now know about both subjects is considerably more than what we knew not very long ago.

Thorough bibliographies of recent work in each topic are Joseph C. Miller's *Slavery: A Comparative Teaching Bibliography* (1977), which the author, in collaboration with others, has brought up to date regularly in the journal *Slavery and Abolition*; and Peter H. Wood's " 'I did the Best I Could for My Day': The Study of Early Black History During the Second Reconstruction, 1960 to 1976," *William and Mary Quarterly*, 3d series, 35 (1978).

To understand why there was a trade of slaves from Africa to the British mainland colonies one must look into reasons for the existence of the "South Atlantic System." Philip D.

Curtin provides the best summary of the history of that system in "The Slave Trade and the Atlantic Basin: Intercontinental Perspectives," in *Key Issues in the Afro-American Past*, vol. 1 (1971), edited by Nathan I. Huggins, Martin L. Kilson, and Daniel M. Fox. Michael Craton's *Sinews of Empire: A Short History of British Slavery* (1974) and Richard S. Dunn's *Sugar and Slaves: The Rise of the Planter Class in the English West Indies, 1624–1715* (1972) are good background for the wider economic realm of the mainland colonies. Curtin's "Epidemiology and the Slave Trade," *Political Science Quarterly*, 83 (1968) discusses the importance of disease factors in decisions to import Africans.

It is difficult to understand what African societies were like before the heavy flow of slaves to the Americas. Even if the Atlantic trade had not altered those societies, Africans did not leave full written records and in many places oral history has fallen short of its promise as a tool for reconstructing the precolonial African past. One wanting an introduction to African ways of life would do well to begin with Philip D. Curtin and Paul Bohannon's *Africa and Africans*, 3d ed. (1988).

Recent studies of slavery in Africa are valuable for discussion of how the institution differed from American chattel slavery and the role it played in the development of slave trading in Africa. Best in this regard is Paul E. Lovejoy's *Transformations in Slavery: A History of Slavery in Africa* (1983), but essays in *Slavery in Africa: Historical and Anthropological Perspectives* (1977), edited by Suzanne Miers and Igor Kopytoff, add useful insight. Lovejoy's article with Martin A. Klein, "Slavery in West Africa," in *The Uncommon Market: Essays in the Economic History of the Atlantic Slave Trade* (1977), edited by Henry A. Gemery and Jan S. Hogendorn, and his "Indigenous African Slavery," *Historical Reflections/ Reflexions historiques*, 4 (1977), provide sharp focus on African slavery as it pertained to the external slave trade.

Discussion of numbers of slaves traded across the Atlantic begins with Philip D. Curtin's pioneering *The Atlantic Slave*

*Trade: A Census* (1969). Before publication of this book, even careful historians tended to cling to a "rounded off" figure of fifteen million for the total of African slave exports, a figure supplied casually in 1861 by an American publicist for Mexican independence, who had no real basis to know. Curtin spent years amassing existing data and arrived at the admittedly tentative estimate of 9,566,100 for slave imports into the Americas between 1451 and 1870. He regarded his book as a "point of departure" and challenged other scholars to produce data revising his figures. What followed was a fairly forceful attack on Curtin's accuracy and methodology. A persistent leader of this criticism, suggesting Curtin seriously underestimated the volume of slave exports, is J. E. Inikori. His initial argument is found in "Measuring the Atlantic Slave Trade: An Assessment of Curtin and Anstey," *Journal of African History*, 17 (1976), to which Curtin replies in the same volume, and a summary of his critique is in Inikori's introduction to his edited work, *Forced Migration: The Impact of the Export Trade on African Societies* (1982). Other scholars, including Roger Anstey in *The Atlantic Slave Trade and British Abolition* (1975), have worked to revise Curtin's figures, and Curtin himself raises parts of his original findings in "Measuring the Atlantic Slave Trade" in *Race and Slavery in the Western Hemisphere: Quantitative Studies* (1975), edited by Stanley L. Engerman and Eugene D. Genovese. The most useful work that sorts through the argument is Paul E. Lovejoy's "The Volume of the Atlantic Slave Trade: A Synthesis," *Journal of African History*, 23 (1982). Lovejoy argues that, after over a decade of challenge and revision, Curtin's original estimates remain close to the mark. A useful addition for slaves imported into the British mainland colonies is Herbert S. Klein, "Slaves and Shipping in Eighteenth-Century Virginia," *Journal of Interdisciplinary Studies*, 5 (1975).

No work on the slave trade to the British colonies on the North American mainland should begin elsewhere than with Elizabeth Donnan's four-volume *Documents Illustrative of the*

*History of the Slave Trade to America* (1930–35). Donnan introduces documents with good material and supports them with full annotations.

The best short study of the Atlantic slave trade is Edward Reynolds's *Stand the Storm: A History of the Atlantic Slave Trade* (1985). James A. Rawley's *The Transatlantic Slave Trade: A History* (1981) is more thorough and treats European aspects of the trade in particular detail. Daniel R. Mannix's *Black Cargoes: A History of the Atlantic Slave Trade, 1518– 1865* (1962) is a moving, popular account. Several books examine the trade and focus on its effects on Africans. English Africanist Basil Davidson's *Black Mother: The Years of the Atlantic Slave Trade* (1961) was the first to draw attention to the destructive nature of the trade for African societies. Two studies by Walter P. Rodney, *A History of the Upper Guinea Coast to 1816* (1968) and *West Africa and the Atlantic Slave Trade* (1967), broaden and advance Davidson's argument. P. E. H. Hair's *The Atlantic Slave Trade and Black Africa* (1978) is a remarkable little book that takes issue with the focus on destructive effects. Hair's work echoes an interpretation expressed more fully by Anthony G. Hopkins in *An Economic History of West Africa* (1973).

Studies of European aspects of the trade often focus on an individual country or colony. Such work on British and colonial American participation includes Walter E. Minchinton's *The Trade of Bristol in the Eighteenth Century* (1966); Richard B. Sheridan's "The Commercial and Financial Organization of the British Slave Trade, 1750–1807," *Economic History Review*, 11 (1958); several articles in *Liverpool, The African Slave Trade, and Abolition: Essays to Illustrate Current Knowledge and Research* (1976), edited by Roger Anstey and P. E. H. Hair; and Jay Coughtry's *The Notorious Triangle: Rhode Island and the Atlantic Slave Trade* (1981). K. G. Davies's *The Royal African Company* (1957) remains the standard for British operations on the African coast in the days of monopoly.

Knowledge of how the slave trade operated along various

sections of the African coast has advanced considerably in recent years with a group of special, regional studies. Among the best for different parts of the coast and related inland areas are Philip D. Curtin's *Economic Change in Precolonial Africa: Senegambia in the Era of the Slave Trade* (1975); Kwame Y. Daaku's *Trade and Politics on the Gold Coast, 1600–1720: A Study of the African Reaction to European Trade* (1970); Ray A. Kea's *Settlements, Trade, and Politics in the Seventeenth-Century Gold Coast* (1982); Patrick Manning's *Slavery, Colonialism, and Economic Growth in Dahomey, 1640–1960* (1982); K. O. Dike's pioneering *Trade and Politics in the Niger Delta* (1956); David Northrup's *Trade Without Rulers: Pre-Colonial Economic Development in South-Eastern Nigeria* (1978); Phyllis Martin's *The External Trade of the Loango Coast* (1972); and two works by Joseph C. Miller, "The Slave Trade in Congo and Angola" in *The African Diaspora: Interpretive Essays* (1976), edited by Martin L. Kilson and Robert I. Rotberg, and his truly monumental *Way of Death: Merchant Capitalism and the Angola Slave Trade, 1780–1830* (1988). Although its focus is on Portuguese slaving in Angola and the middle passage to Brazil, if a person could read but one book to understand the operation of the Atlantic slave trade and to get a sense of its horrors, *Way of Death* should be it.

Paul E. Lovejoy's *Caravans of Kola: The Hausa Kola Trade, 1700–1900* (1980) is good for organization of caravans in the Central Sudan. Philip D. Curtin's *Cross-Cultural Trade in World History* (1984) has useful chapters on trading communities and such topics as landlords, brokers, and caravan leaders in western Africa.

For a number of years, study of the middle passage rested on contemporary accounts, some of which were published. The best examples are John Newton's *The Journal of a Slave Trader, 1750–1754* (1962), edited by Bernard Martin and Mark Spurrell, and Alexander Falconbridge's *An Account of the Slave Trade on the Coast of Africa* (1788). But recently a group of economists and historians began examining statistical data to provide evidence for their conclusions on the voyage between

Africa and America. Herbert S. Klein's *The Middle Passage: Comparative Studies in the Atlantic Slave Trade* (1978) is a fascinating volume that compares a host of aspects of the trade of different nations. An excellent study of disease environments, epidemics, and medical practices as they relate to the middle passage is Richard B. Sheridan's *Doctors and Slaves: A Medical and Demographic History of Slavery in the British West Indies, 1680–1834* (1985). Joseph C. Miller argues that factors in Africa—drought or cycles of harvest, for example—affected mortality in the middle passage in his "Mortality in the Atlantic Slave Trade: Evidence on Causality," *Journal of Interdisciplinary History* (1981). Raymond L. Cohn and Richard A. Jensen's "The Determinants of Slave Mortality Rates on the Middle Passage," *Explorations in Economic History*, 19 (1982), argues that "profit-maximizing behavior" on the part of shipowners and captains made mortality rates higher on slaving voyages than others. David Eltis's "Free and Coerced Migrants: Some Comparisons," *American Historical Review*, 88 (1983), stresses similarities between the two groups.

Among the rare, first-hand accounts of African slaves are those of two kidnapping victims and one person captured by an enemy army, all from the eighteenth century. These are Olaudah Equiano's *Interesting Narrative of the Life of Olaudah Equiano, or Gustavus Vassa, the African, Written by Himself* (1789), edited by Paul Edwards (1967); Ayuba Suleiman Diallo's *Some Memories of the Life of Job, the Son of Solomon the High Priest of Boonda in Africa* (1734), treated recently in Douglas Grant, *The Fortunate Slave: An Illustration of African Slavery in the Eighteenth Century* (1968); and Venture Smith, *A Narrative of the Life and Adventures of Venture, A Native of Africa but Resident about Sixty Years in the United States of America* (1798). The first two of these receive excellent treatment in Philip D. Curtin's *Africa Remembered: Narratives of West Africans from the Era of the Slave Trade* (1967).

Control of economic power and resources in the English mainland colonies affected sale of slaves there. Thus, the clearest discussions of sale and transportation of slaves are in studies that deal with colonial society and slavery. The best of these studies are discussed in the next section, below. Studies of particular colonial ports and importing regions are especially useful. For Charleston, where more slaves entered than at any other port, compare W. Robert Higgins's "Charleston: Terminus and Entrepôt of the Colonial Slave Trade" in *The African Diaspora* with Elizabeth Donnan's "The Slave Trade into South Carolina Before the Revolution," *American Historical Review*, 33 (1928), and Daniel C. Littlefield's, "Charleston and Internal Slave Redistribution," *South Carolina Historical Magazine* (1986). For other areas see Darold D. Wax's "Black Immigrants: The Slave Trade in Colonial Maryland," *Maryland History Magazine*, 73 (1978); Wax's "Africans on the Delaware: The Pennsylvania Slave Trade," *Pennsylvania History*, 50 (1983); and James G. Lyndon's "New York and the Slave Trade, 1700–1774," *William and Mary Quarterly*, 3d series, 35 (1978).

Because slavery in the mainland colonies was so thoroughly involved with the economic situation of the colonies and their quest for laborers to produce exports, study of the origins of slavery and racism in America might well begin with *The Economy of British America, 1607–1789* (1985) by John J. McCusker and Russell R. Menard. The latter is a student of slavery in colonial Maryland, and, among other things, the book reflects his interest in and knowledge about early slavery in the colonies. Other good beginnings are the thoughtful examination of the development of colonial society in Gary B. Nash's excellent synthesis, *Red, White, and Black: The Peoples of Early America*, 2d ed. (1982); and Wesley F. Craven's essays in *White, Red, and Black: The Seventeenth-Century Virginian* (1971). Raymond Starr's bibliographic essay on the subject, "History and the Origins of British North American Slavery," *Historian*, 36 (1973), is good if now dated; Sylvia R. Frey's "In Search of Roots: The Colonial Antecedents of Slavery in the Plantation Colonies," *The Georgia Historical Quarterly*, 68 (1984), covers more recent work.

Modern studies of the origin of slavery in the English mainland colonies often trace their roots to an article by Oscar and Mary Handlin, "Origins of the Southern Labor System," *William and Mary Quarterly*, 3d series, 7 (1950). The authors argue that black slavery evolved over the seventeenth century because of the colonies' labor needs that the colonists could not meet otherwise. According to the Handlins, black and white servants in the colonies received similar treatment and were unconcerned with color. Racial prejudice came after, and as a result of, enslavement. This argument appeared at a fortunate time for interest in black American history. Kenneth Stampp made the Handlins' interpretation popular in his widely read *The Peculiar Institution: Slaves in the Ante-Bellum South* (1956).

Soon, however, a counterargument appeared. In "Slavery and the Genesis of American Race Prejudice," *Comparative Studies of History and Society*, 2 (1959), Carl N. Degler suggests that racist ideologies preceded and played a major role in bringing about slavery. As the legal system of slavery evolved in the Chesapeake, Degler writes, "it reflected and included as part of its essence, the same discrimination which white men had practiced against the Negro all along." Thomas F. Gossett strengthened Degler's arguments in *Race: A History of an Idea in America* (1963). It remained for Winthrop D. Jordan to attempt resolution of the debate in *White Over Black: American Attitudes Toward the Negro, 1550–1812* (1968). Jordan calls the move to black slavery an "unthinking decision" and suggests "cause and effect" for the relationship between slavery and racism. Gary B. Nash summarizes many of the arguments clearly in "Red, White, and Black: The Origins of Racism in Colonial America," in *The Great Fear: Race in the Mind of America* (1970), edited by Nash and Richard Weiss.

Nearly two decades of focus on the issues, reinforced by national attention on civil rights toward the end of the 1960s, stimulated further investigation into colonial slavery and the early development of the institution. Many studies focused naturally on the Chesapeake, where slavery first appeared and became most thoroughly established through the first century of English rule of the North American mainland. Thad W. Tate's "The Seventeenth-Century Chesapeake and Its Modern Historians" in *The Chesapeake in the Seventeenth Century: Essays on Anglo-American Society* (1979), edited by Thad W. Tate and David L. Ammerman, surveys this literature; Anita H. Rutman's "Still Planting the Seeds of Hope: The Recent Literature of the Early Chesapeake Region," *The Virginia Magazine of History and Biography*, 95 (1987) is a critical examination of more current work.

One of the freshest approaches to appear in the 1970s was Edmund S. Morgan's *American Slavery, American Freedom: The Ordeal of Colonial Virginia* (1975). Morgan regards as especially important the need in the last third of the seventeenth century for control of unruly, armed, freed white servants. Slaves could never be freed, could be more carefully controlled, and were thus preferable to white servants. Russell R. Menard takes issue with Morgan in "From Servants to Slaves: The Transformation of the Chesapeake Labor System," *Southern Studies*, 16 (1977). Basing his study on work conducted for his University of Iowa doctoral thesis, eventually published as *Economy and Society in Early Colonial Maryland* (1985), Menard argues that the rise of black slavery was due principally to the change in white servant migration patterns after 1660 and the high cost of servants in comparison with the low cost of slaves. "Chesapeake planters did not abandon indentured servitude," Menard writes. "It abandoned them."

More recent studies add evidence for standard arguments about slavery's beginnings in America, but a number of them include thorough study of black society and slave culture in the Chesapeake. Gloria L. Main supports the idea that opting for slavery was a rational economic choice in *Tobacco Colony: Life in Early Maryland, 1650–1720* (1982). Main documents the social life and material culture of all classes of early Mary-landers with study in probate records from six Maryland counties. She shows that the institutionalization of slavery hastened permanent inequality in the colony. This last point is one Allan Kulikoff makes in *Tobacco and Slaves: The Development of Southern Culture in the Chesapeake, 1680–1800* (1986). Guided by interest in class formation, Kulikoff focuses on the rise of a Chesapeake gentry and its co-optation of a yeoman class to solidify white control over economy, society, and government. Once whites united under leadership of the gentry, Kulikoff argues, the status of blacks as a permanent underclass, with slavery as its outward manifestation, was established as the basis of southern culture.

Other recent studies use some of the same kinds of sources to reach different conclusions. T. H. Breen and Stephen Innes's *'Myne Owne Ground': Race and Freedom on Virginia's Eastern Shore, 1640–1676* (1980) focuses on successful free blacks and their broad social and economic relations. The authors conclude that the loss of property rights moved blacks swiftly toward a more permanent position of slavery. Paul G. E. Clemens's *Atlantic Economy and Colonial Maryland's Eastern Shore: From Tobacco to Grain* (1980) looks to the effect of wheat production after 1713 on the changing social order. Darrett B. Rutman and Anita H. Rutman's *A Place in Time: Middlesex County, Virginia, 1650–1750* (1984) analyzes everything from child-naming patterns to literacy and slaves' living conditions in a single Virginia population. For the beginnings of slavery the Rutmans conclude that, on the local level, individual choice and good or bad fortune played surprisingly important roles. Philip J. Schwarz's *Twice Condemned: Slaves and the Criminal Laws of Virginia, 1705–1865* (1988) examines trials of slaves to prove how conflict and brutality were so much at the heart of the relationship between white and black in colonial Virginia.

If early slavery in South Carolina and the Georgia low country has not commanded a quantity of attention equal to that in the Chesapeake, those books that have focused on the subject have been of considerable quality. Two studies each dominate recent work on blacks in colonial South Carolina and Georgia. Peter H. Wood's *Black Majority: Negroes in Colonial South Carolina from 1670 through the Stono Rebellion* (1974) treats origins and development of slavery as well as the formation of black culture in the colony. Everything from black pioneers in the early eighteenth century to the evolution of Gullah speech comes under Wood's scrutiny. Daniel Littlefield's *Rice and Slaves: Ethnicity and the Slave Trade in Colonial South Carolina* (1981) is a different kind of book, examining rice production in particular and the African ethnic mix that provided much to white South Carolina as it formed its own, separate subculture. An article by John S. Otto and Nain E. Anderson, "The Origins of Southern Cattle-Grazing: A Problem in West Indian History," *Journal of Caribbean History*, 21 (1988), argues that decades of cultural interchange among Africans, Hispanics, and Britons brought about the special techniques of cattle grazing in colonial South Carolina that later spread throughout the South.

For Georgia, Betty Wood's *Slavery in Colonial Georgia, 1730–1770* (1984) is especially good for the period of Georgia's social experiment, when planter pressures brought about the demise of the ideal colony. Wood devotes the second half of the book to the form of slavery that came to exist in Georgia up to the time of the Revolution, with particularly good chapters on the public and private lives of slaves. Julia Floyd Smith's *Slavery and Rice Culture in Low Country Georgia, 1750–1860* (1985) is interesting for its perspective. Smith believes slavery on rice plantations in Georgia was different from other manifestations of the institution in America. Rice production had its own requirements for labor, in particular a task system for fieldwork. This setting, Smith argues, enabled low-country blacks to develop a culture with more African elements in the mix and to enjoy physical well-being and general treatment that was better than slaves experienced elsewhere.

Because of its relatively small number of blacks and because states in the region terminated slavery around the time cotton production began to boom in the Deep South, historians have tended to overlook New England and the Middle Colonies in the field of slave studies. Indicative of this is the existence of only a few new monographs on the subject over the last two decades.

A solid, general treatment of the topic is Edgar J. Mc-Manus's *Black Bondage in the North* (1973), which follows the story past Emancipation. Lorenzo J. Greene's *The Negro in Colonial New England* (1942) remains standard for the topic. The book has a massive bibliography and useful appendices with population figures for each colony. A refreshing new study of blacks in New England is William D. Piersen's *Black Yankees: The Development of an Afro-American Sub-culture in Eighteenth-Century New England* (1988), which focuses less on the institution of slavery and more on "what it was like to be an African immigrant in colonial New England." Piersen examines African American folk culture in religion, rituals, arts and crafts, folklore, social mores, and daily behavior, concluding that in spite of being "engulfed in a pervasive, narrow-minded Euro-American society that had no interest in fostering Afro-American autonomy," blacks in New England created a viable folk culture that maintained African values and gave blacks a positive identity. Bernard Steiner's *History of Slavery in Connecticut* (1893) and William Johnston's *Slavery in Rhode Island, 1755–1776* (1894) have not been superseded. Robert P. Twombly and Robert H. Moore's "Black Puritan: The Negro in Seventeenth-Century Massachusetts," *William and Mary Quarterly*, 3d series, 24 (1967), addresses the atypical situation of blacks in the Puritan colony.

Studies of African Americans in other colonies include Edgar J. McManus's *A History of Negro Slavery in New York* (1966) and two older but still useful works: Henry S. Cooley's *A Study of Slavery in New Jersey* (1896) and Edward J. Turner's *The Negro in Pennsylvania: Slavery–Servitude–Freedom* (1911). Several articles by Darold D. Wax in *Pennsylvania History*—including "Negro Imports into Pennsylvania, 1720–1766," 32 (1965), and "The Demand for Slave Labor in Colonial Pennsylvania," 32 (1967)—are useful. Thomas E. Drake's *Quakers and Slavery in America* (1950) treats the controversy about Quakers and the slave trade in Pennsylvania. Allan Tully offers interesting information on slaveholding in rural Pennsylvania in "Patterns of Slaveholding in Colonial Pennsylvania: Chester and Lancaster Counties, 1729–1758," *Journal of Social History*, 6 (1973).

There has been so much focus on slaves as agricultural workers that historians have tended to overlook the varied experiences of blacks in northern colonial cities. Two exceptions are Thomas J. Archdeacon's *New York City, 1664–1710: Conquest and Change* (1976), which includes information on numbers and residence patterns of blacks in that city, and two works by Gary B. Nash, his "Slaves and Slaveowners in Colonial Philadelphia" in his *Race, Class, and Politics: Essays on American Colonial and Revolutionary Society* (1986), and his newer *Forging Freedom: The Formation of Philadelphia's Black Community, 1720–1840* (1988). Nash's pieces show that even the presence of strong abolitionist sentiment among Quakers and others in the city had little effect when Philadelphia residents wanted slaves to work for them.

For studies of Africans and slavery among the Spanish and French in North America, see Leslie B. Rout, Jr.'s *The African Experience in Spanish America: 1502 to the Present Day* (1976); Joe Gray Taylor's *Negro Slavery in Louisiana* (1963); and Daniel H. Usner, Jr.'s "From African Captivity to American Slavery: The Introduction of Black Laborers to Colonial Louisiana," *Louisiana History*, 20 (1979).

Ira Berlin's "Time, Space, and the Evolution of Afro-American Society on British Mainland North America," *American Historical Review*, 85 (1980), is the best introduction to black culture in the colonial period. In emphasizing the importance of an evolutionary process in African acculturation, which differed according to place, Berlin has jarred historians loose from any idea that colonial black culture was mostly alike and static. T. H. Breen's "Creative Adaptations: Peoples and Cultures" and Gary B. Nash's "Social Development" in *Colonial British America: Essays in the New History of the*

*Early Modern Era* (1984), edited by Jack P. Greene and J. R. Pole, are good introductions to Africian American acculturation and community development.

The best studies of African American acculturation in the New World have been anthropological works focusing on slave societies in the Caribbean. What they say about how the process takes place is instructive for colonial America. Melville Herskovits's *The Myth of the Negro Past* (1941) is the classic study of "creolization"; Sidney W. Mintz's *Caribbean Transformations* (1974) and Mintz and Richard Price's *An Anthropological Approach to the Afro-American Past: A Caribbean Perspective* (1976) offer valuable new ideas about the joining of cultures.

Although most books on slave community and culture focus on the antebellum period, good introductions to the topic, with some references to earlier times, include Lawrence W. Levine's *Black Culture and Black Consciousness: Afro-American Folk Thought from Slavery to Freedom* (1977); Eugene D. Genovese's *Roll, Jordan, Roll: The World the Slaves Made* (1972); and John W. Blassingame's *The Slave Community: Plantation Life in the Antebellum South*, revised (1977). The studies of blacks in specific regions of colonial America noted above—particularly those by Gloria Main, Allan Kulikoff, Darrett and Anita Rutman, Peter Wood, Daniel Littlefield, Betty Wood, Julia Floyd Smith, Lorenzo Green, and William Piersen—have useful parts on black community and culture. Kulikoff's book emphasizes the role demographics played in black family and community formation and shows how these institutions were the prerequisites for stable black culture in the Chesapeake. Agreeing generally with Kulikoff's demographic analysis is Russell R. Menard's "The Maryland Slave Population: A Demographic Profile of Blacks in Four Counties," *William and Mary Quarterly*, 3d series, 32 (1975). Jean Butendoff Lee's "The Problem of Slave Community in the Eighteenth-Century Chesapeake," *William and Mary Quarterly*, 3d series, 43 (1986), questions assumptions about the existence of a stable African American community by the time of the Revolutionary era. She recognizes the broad attempts of slaves to achieve communal lives, but emphasizes these efforts were more difficult and often less successful than many historians believe. *The Diary of Landon Carter of Sabine Hall, 1752–1778*, 2 vols. (1965), edited by Jack P. Greene, contains insight into the way one not altogether typical planter thought of and related to his slaves.

Two recent publications provide refreshing perspectives on colonial black culture in different sections of the British mainland. Mechal Sobel's *The World They Made Together: Black and White Values in Eighteenth-Century Virginia* (1987) examines religious and secular values and finds that black and white values and perceptions had considerable effect on one another's group culture. Sobel ventures into the fascinating realm of black and white concepts of space, time, home, the afterlife, and more to suggest that neither group developed its culture alone, but that indeed they made their worlds together. Piersen's *Black Yankees* makes a similar argument. He concludes that blacks helped "mellow those rather puritanical" white Yankees.

E. Franklin Frazier's *The Negro Family in the United States* (1939), which emphasizes the damage slavery did to the black family, was a standard work on the subject. However, Herbert G. Gutman's *The Black Family in Slavery and Freedom, 1750–1925* (1976) altered ideas that slavery brought disorganization and instability to black families. Gutman draws attention to the remarkable adaptive capacities of African Americans, and he credits the black family with preserving cultural traditions and the double-headed household. Most of Gutman's evidence is from the antebellum period and after, but he has a chapter on the family in the eighteenth century in which he deals with African American marriage and broadening kinship ties. Allan Kulikoff's "The Beginnings of the Afro-American Family in Maryland" in *Law, Society, and Politics in Early Maryland: Essays in Honor of Morris Leon Radoff* (1976), edited by Aubrey C. Land, Lois Green Carr, and Edward C. Papenfuse, summarizes Kulikoff's thoughts on demographic considerations and the formation of colonial black families. Mary Beth Norton, Herbert G. Gutman, and Ira Berlin's "The Afro-American Family in the Age of Revolution" in *Slavery and Freedom in the Age of the American Revolution* (1983), edited by Berlin and Ronald Hoffman, examines the workings of slave families in the Chesapeake and the Carolinas in a more mature African American society.

Because many agree with Michael R. Bradley's assessment in "The Role of the Black Church in Colonial Slave Society," *Louisiana Studies*, 14 (1975), "that the formation of the Negro church is the key to the beginning of Afro-American community and culture," a number of studies have focused on the early years of black religion in America. Several noted historians have written good books on African American religion. These include Carter G. Woodson's *History of the Negro Church* (1921); Benjamin E. Mays and Joseph W. Nicholson's *The Negro's Church* (1933); and E. Franklin Frazier's shorter *The Negro Church in America* (1963). Lester B. Scherer's *Slavery and the Churches in Early America, 1619–1819* (1975) treats the colonial period more thoroughly; David M. Reimers's *White Protestantism and the Negro* (1965) has a portion on conversion and church origins.

Works that deal with particular denominations and blacks in early America include Donald G. Mathews, *Slavery and Methodism: A Chapter in American Morality, 1780–1845* (1965); T. Erskine Clark, "An Experiment in Paternalism: Presbyterians and Slaves in Charleston, South Carolina," *Journal of Presbyterian History*, 53 (1975); and Denzil T. Clifton, "Anglicanism and Negro Slavery in Colonial America," *Historical Magazine of the Protestant Episcopal Church*, 39 (1970). Harold E. Davis's *The Fledgling Province: Social and Cultural Life in Colonial Georgia, 1733–1776* (1976) argues that Quakers and Moravians wanted their slaves to become literate so they could experience Christianity more fully. Davis maintains that churches in colonial Georgia were more integrated than previously believed. Mechal Sobel's *Trabelin' On: The Slave*

*Journey to an Afro-Baptist Faith* (1979) includes ideas on acculturation as they pertain to the formation of African American religions. Sobel's is the most thorough treatment of the "African Sacred Cosmos" and of how such African concepts as spiritual force, visions, travels to meet the Lord, and rebirth entered into the African American Christian world view. Leonard Barrett's *Soul Force: African Heritage in Afro-American Religion* (1974) shows how other Africanisms mingled with European Christianity in the formative years of black religion in America. Alan Gallay's "Planters and Slaves in the Great Awakening" in *Masters and Slaves in the House of the Lord: Race and Religion in the American South, 1740–1870* (1988), edited by John B. Boles, argues that the Great Awakening had more effect on slave society, especially in South Carolina and Georgia after the 1740s, than previously thought. Carol V. R. George offers a modern treatment of Richard Allen and the birth of the Bethel African Methodist Episcopal Church in *Segregated Sabbaths: Richard Allen and the Emergence of Independent Black Churches* (1973).

Herbert Aptheker's *American Negro Slave Revolts*, revised (1969), remains the most thorough compilation of information on the subject. The best analysis of how and why slaves resisted, ran away, or rebelled is Gerald W. Mullin's *Flight and Rebellion: Slave Resistance in Eighteenth-Century Virginia* (1972). Mullin establishes the relationship between level of acculturation and methods of resistance that seemed to apply throughout the colonial period. Studies of particular topics related to resistance or rebellion include Thomas J. Davis's *A Rumor of Revolt: The Great Negro Plot in Colonial New York* (1985), which argues the plot was more than rumor and that "slaves in New York City during 1741 clearly talked of doing damage to the society enslaving them"; John J. TePaske's "The Fugitive Slave: Intercolonial Rivalry and Spanish Slave Policy, 1686–1764" in *Eighteenth-Century Florida and Its Borderlands* (1975), edited by Samuel Proctor; Jeffery J. Crow's "Slave Rebelliousness and Social Conflict in North Carolina,

1775–1802," *William and Mary Quarterly*, 3d series, 37 (1980); and Darold D. Wax's "Negro Resistance to the Early American Slave Trade," *Journal of Negro History*, 46 (1961).

If work dominated the daily lives of African Americans in the colonial period, blacks dominated the colonial American world of work—for whites as well as blacks. One gets this strong impression from reading the studies of blacks in the colonial era noted earlier, no more so than in Sobel's *The World They Made Together*. The best short introduction to slaves' work in all the British mainland colonies is Richard S. Dunn's "Servants and Slaves: The Recruitment and Employment of Labor" in *Colonial British America*. Studies of specific kinds of African American workers include Philip D. Morgan's "Work and Culture: The Task System and the World of Lowcountry Blacks, 1700–1880," *William and Mary Quarterly*, 3d series, 40 (1982), which shows how greatly the task system affected the black and white worlds of the South Carolina and Georgia low country; Morgan's "Black Life in Eighteenth-Century Charleston," *Perspectives in American History*, new series, 1 (1984), a detailed description of living and working conditions of urban slaves; Thad W. Tate's *The Negro in Eighteenth-Century Williamsburg* (1965), for the lives and kinds of work of African Americans in the setting of a town; Sarah S. Hughes's, "Slaves for Hire: The Allocation of Black Labor in Elizabeth City County, Virginia, 1787–1810," *William and Mary Quarterly*, 3d series, 35 (1978); and Ronald L. Lewis's *Coal, Iron, and Slaves: Industrial Slavery in Maryland and Virginia, 1715–1865* (1979).

That black women had especially full lives of hard work as slaves is evident in Joan Rezner Gundersen's "The Double Bonds of Race and Sex: Black and White Women in a Colonial Virginia Parish," *Journal of Southern History*, 52 (1986). Gundersen reminds readers that black women on small farms often had to do their own domestic work after the fieldwork was over. She shows also that in part of Virginia women were hired out more frequently than men. Deborah Gray White's *Ar'n't I A Woman: Female Slaves in the Plantation South*

(1985) contains a description of the mythology of female slavery as well as select information on black women in the colonial period. Other studies of women in slavery focus heavily on the antebellum South, but see Angela Davis's "Reflections on the Black Woman's Role in the Community of Slaves," *The Black Scholar*, 3 (1971), for a theoretical approach; Catherine Clinton's *The Plantation Mistress: Woman's World in the Old South* (1982), which is especially good for "the sexual dynamics of slavery"; and Suzanne Lebsock's *The Free Women of Petersburg: Status and Culture in a Southern Town, 1784–1860* (1984) for the chapter on "Free Women of Color."

Historians of African Americans are only beginning to rely on the work of archaeologists for study of the material culture of pre-Revolutionary slaves, but work is progressing rapidly. Examples of the value of archaeological studies are William M. Kelso's *Kingsmill Plantations, 1619–1800: Archaeology of Country Life in Colonial Virginia* (1984); *Archaeology of Slavery and Plantation Life* (1985), edited by Theresa A. Singleton; and Singleton's "Breaking New Ground," *Southern Exposure*, 15 (1988). Kelso provides details of the slave quarters, gardens, wells, pots, root cellars, and garbage pits, and from this information he infers much about slave living conditions.

Some of the most enlightening work of the past decade has to do with health, nutrition, disease, and medical practice in the slave community. Kenneth F. Kiple and Virginia Himmelsteib King's *Another Dimension of the Black Diaspora: Diet, Disease, and Racism* (1981) is the most valuable for the colonial period. The authors discuss African immunities, New World epidemics related to the Atlantic trade, and blacks' particular susceptibility to disease because of nutritional deficiencies and special problems of transplanted tropical Africans. Todd L. Savitt's *Medicine and Slavery: The Diseases and Health Care of Blacks in Antebellum Virginia* (1978) reinforces many of Kiple and King's conclusions with a clearer nineteenth-century focus. Tom W. Shick's "Healing and Race in the Carolina Low Country" in *Africans in Bondage: Studies in Slavery and the Slave Trade* (1986), edited by Paul E.

Lovejoy, describes black "root doctors" and their holistic approach to healing. Gary Puckrein's "Climate, Health, and Black Labor in English America," *Journal of American Studies*, 13 (1979), argues that the white idea that African Americans could live longer under conditions of hard labor in tropical climes—in spite of there being no clear evidence at the time that it was so—was a factor in landowners' decisions to turn to Africa for slave labor.

Until recently, study of African Americans in the era of the American Revolution was one of the most neglected areas of African American history. This was especially true if one wanted to know what happened in the period to blacks who were not participants in the war. Studies that existed tended to examine the broad effects of Revolutionary sentiment on the institution of slavery, without attention to the lot of black people in the country through those years. For this reason, one of the most valuable recent additions to African American history is *Slavery and Freedom in the Age of the American Revolution* (1983), edited by Ira Berlin and Ronald Hoffman. Berlin's "The Revolution in Black Life" in *The American Revolution: Explorations in the History of American Radicalism* (1976), edited by Alfred F. Young, is a good introduction to the subject.

Two books by David B. Davis, *The Problem of Slavery in Western Culture* (1966) and *The Problem of Slavery in the Age of Revolution, 1770–1823* (1975) are standard treatments of the broad range of issues connecting slavery with Western and libertarian ideology. Jordan's *White Over Black* is a thorough treatment of some of the same topics.

Arthur Zilversmit's *The First Emancipation: The Abolition of Slavery in the North* (1967) argues that idealism prevailed over economic interest to end slavery north of Maryland. One should supplement it with Robin Blackburn's *The Overthrow of Colonial Slavery, 1776–1848* (1988). *The Journal of John Woolman* (1775) is good for understanding the strong Quaker sentiment against slavery. Elaine MacEacheren's

"Emancipation of Slaves in Massachusetts: A Reexamination, 1770–1790," *Journal of Negro History*, 55 (1970), puts *Commonwealth* v. *Jenison* in perspective. Robert W. Fogel and Stanley L. Engerman's "Philanthropy at Bargain Prices: Notes on the Economics of Gradual Emancipation," *Journal of Legal Studies*, 13 (1974), shows how arrival of white immigrants provided northern states an adequate labor supply and made adherence to ideals and gradual emancipation possible. Also useful is Donald L. Robinson's *Slavery and the Struggle for American Politics, 1765–1820* (1971).

Where slavery fit into Thomas Jefferson's thinking is the subject of John C. Miller's *The Wolf by the Ears: Thomas Jefferson and Slavery* (1977), which one should supplement with Fawn Brodie's *Thomas Jefferson: An Intimate Biography* (1974) and William Cohen's "Thomas Jefferson and the Problem of Slavery," *Journal of American History*, 56 (1969).

The origins and growth of the free black population in the upper South are covered thoroughly in Ira Berlin's *Slaves Without Masters: The Free Negro in the Antebellum South* (1974). John Hope Franklin's *The Free Negro in North Carolina, 1790–1860* (1943) is a detailed study of the "unwanted people" in that state. Sidney Kaplan's *The Black Presence in the Era of the American Revolution* (1973) includes treatment of a number of free blacks whose accomplishments were extraordinary.

The most thorough study of black participation in the Revolutionary struggle is Benjamin Quarles's *The Negro in the American Revolution* (1961). Sylvia R. Frey's "Between Slavery and Freedom: Virginia Blacks in the American Revolution," *Journal of Southern History*, 49 (1983), covers British attempts to lure away Virginia slaves, showing the strength of the British appeal and the unhealthy living conditions for those who ran off to British armies. Peter H. Wood's " 'The Dream Deferred': Black Freedom Struggles on the Eve of White Independence" in *In Resistance: Studies in African, Caribbean, and Afro-American History* (1986), edited by Gary Y. Okihiro, is an examination of the wave of hope and discontent that welled up among African Americans between 1765 and 1776. American blacks manifested these feelings in serious efforts of resistance and a struggle to free themselves from slavery that culminated in death and disappointment in 1775–76. Good supplements are Luther P. Jackson's "Virginia Negro Soldiers and Seamen in the American Revolution," *Journal of Negro History*, 27 (1942), and Pete Maslowski's "National Policy Toward Use of Black Troops in the Revolution," *South Carolina Historical Magazine*, 73 (1972). For the fate of blacks who left with the British see James W. Walker's *The Black Loyalists: The Search for a Promised Land in Nova Scotia and Sierra Leone, 1783–1870* (1976) or Ellen Gibson Wilson's *The Loyal Blacks* (1976), the source for the section in chapter 4 on Boston King.

Articles by Gary B. Nash, Richard S. Dunn, Philip D. Morgan, and Allan Kulikoff in *Slavery and Freedom in the Age of the American Revolution* trace changes in black society in various regions through the period. Kulikoff's *Tobacco and Slaves* is good to read with Dunn's article for social change in the Chesapeake and for implications of this change in the antebellum period. Duncan J. MacLeod's *Slavery, Race and the American Revolution* (1974) argues the importance of the Revolutionary era for the establishment of racism in America. Staughton Lynd's *Class Conflict, Slavery, and the United States Constitution* (1967); Edmund S. Morgan's "Conflict and Consensus in the American Revolution" in *Essays on the American Revolution* (1973), edited by Stephen G. Katz and James H. Hutson; and Richard R. Beeman's *The Evolution of the Southern Backcountry: A Case Study of Lunenburg County, Virginia, 1746–1832* (1984) are provocative studies that relate to the topic. Fredrika Teute Schmidt and Barbara Ripel Wilhelm's "Early Proslavery Petitions in Virginia," *William and Mary Quarterly*, 3d series, 30 (1973), shows the strength of proslavery sentiment in Virginia through times when there was a push for manumission. F. Nwabueze Okoye's "Chattel Slavery as the Nightmare of the American Revolutionaries," *William and Mary Quarterly*, 3d series, 37 (1980), is critical of the "establishment historians" who have underplayed the importance of race and slavery to the colonial pamphleteers. William W. Freehling's "The Founding Fathers and Slavery," *American Historical Review*, 77 (1972), also is useful.

More specific studies that relate to the topic include Robert McColley's *Slavery and Jeffersonian Virginia*, 2d ed. (1973); Jeffrey J. Crow's *The Black Experience in Revolutionary North Carolina* (1977); Frances D. Pingeon's "Slavery in New Jersey on the Eve of the Revolution" in *New Jersey in the American Revolution*, revised (1974), edited by William C. Wright; and chapters by Mary Beth Norton on southern women in the Revolution, Michael Mullin on British Caribbean and mainland slaves through the war, and Peter H. Wood on republicanism and slave society in South Carolina in *The Southern Experience in the American Revolution*, edited by Jeffrey J. Crow and Larry E. Tise (1978).

# INDEX

Byrd, William, 94

Cabinda (slave-trading port), 31
Calabar (slave-trading port), 30
Campbell, William, Lord: 129
Canada, 124
capitalism, 118
caravans, slave-trading: 26, 28, 30, 31, 32–33, 36
Caribbean, 8
Carter, Landon, 103
Carter, Robert "King," 6, 44, 79
Charleston, South Carolina, 44, 63, 67, 68, 88, 101, 102, 106, 115, 129, 134, 135, 136, 141
Charlestown, Rhode Island, 74
Chesapeake Region, 1, 18, 34, 44, 46–47, 54, 55, 58–60, 87–88, 107–108, 109, 125–129. *See also* Maryland, Virginia
childbearing, 105–106
child rearing, 94
children, in slave trade: 40
Christianity, 84, 95–98, 128, 139–140, 145
Church, African American: 133, 139–140, 148, 151
cities, 70, 100, 102, 132, 133, 144, 148, 150. *See also* individual cities; slaves, in urban areas
Civil War, 150
climate, of Virginia, 49
Clinton, Henry, General: 127
clothing, of slaves: 110–111
colonists, English: 46–54, 99, 117–118
  Salzburger, 118
  Scottish, 118
*Commonwealth* v. *Jennison*, 125
communities, African American: 3, 4, 82–91, 98, 141, 142, 147, 151
  in cities, 132, 133, 138, 140
  commercial (on African coast), 26
*Compagnie des Indies*, 20n
Company of Royal Adventurers, 24
competition, at African ports: 36
compromises, in United States Constitution: 145–146

Congo-Angola (slave-trading region), 11, 26, 31–32
Congress, United States: 149
"conjurers," 113
Connecticut, 74, 75, 114, 125
conspiracies, of slaves: 75, 101, 129
Constitution, of United States: 117, 120, 145–146, 150
Constitutional Convention, 145
Constitutions, of states: 124, 125
Continental Congress, 120, 136
corn (maize), 104
Cornwallis, Charles, Lord: 135
cotton, 137, 141, 149
creoles (slaves born in America), 87, 88, 89, 106, 138, 141, 142
crew, on slave ships: 35
Crow, Jeffrey J., 129
culture, African American: 3, 4, 82–115, 130, 134, 137, 140, 142, 151
  in Chesapeake, 87–88
  in Low Country, 69, 88–89
  in New England and Middle Colonies, 89–9
  Euro-American: 115
cultures, of western Africa: 82, 83
Curaçao, 71
currencies, in slave trading: 37
Curtin, Philip D., 17, 26, 33
"custom," payment of (in western Africa): 35–36

Dahomey (western African state), 30
dance, African American: 114
Davies, Samuel, 98
Davis, David Brion, 118–119
Declaration of Independence, 116, 120
Delaware, 72, 140
de Laussat, Pierre, 114
demography, and African American acculturation: 84–86, 91
  of English colonial America, 48
diet, in Africa, 33
  in middle passage, 41–42
  of slaves in America, 111–112
Dinah (slave of Robert Carter), 79

*African Americans in the Colonial Era: From African Origins through the American Revolution* was copyedited by Andrew J. Davidson. Production editor was Lucy Herz. Martha Urban proofread the copy. The text was typeset by Impressions, Inc., and printed and bound by Edwards Brothers, Inc. Maps were prepared by James A. Bier.

The cover and text were designed by Roger Eggers.